JOHN MITCHEL, ULSTER AND THE GREAT IRISH FAMINE

JOHN MITCHEL, ULSTER AND THE GREAT IRISH FAMINE

Edited by

Patrick Fitzgerald and Anthony Russell

Irish Academic Press

First published in 2017 by
Irish Academic Press
10 George's Street
Newbridge
Co. Kildare
Ireland
www.iap.ie

9781911024668 (Paper)
9781911024705 (Kindle)
9781911024682 (Epub)
9781911024699 (PDF)

British Library Cataloguing in Publication Data
An entry can be found on request

Library of Congress Cataloging in Publication Data
An entry can be found on request

Interior design by www.jminfotechindia.com
Typeset in 11/14 Minion Pro

Cover design by edit+ www.stuartcoughlan.com
Cover front: Courtesy of Ireland's Great Hunger Museum,
Quinnipiac University, Hamden, CT

CONTENTS

Acknowledgements

The editors wish to express their thanks to Mr John O'Hare and the Clanrye Trust without whose support neither this publication nor the four-day 2015 International Famine Conference would have been possible.

Introduction

Patrick Fitzgerald and Anthony Russell

This collection of essays is based on research presented at the annual Great Famine Commemoration in 2015, when it crossed the border to be held in Northern Ireland for the first time. The symbolism of this should not be lost on any of us, and the editors firmly hope that this book will help facilitate a more inclusive and appropriate remembering of famine in our history.

An ever-present figure during our deliberations in September 2015 was Newry resident John Mitchel. Whatever else might be said of Mitchel, we can assuredly present him as a complex and multi-faceted figure around whom controversy seemed to swirl relentlessly. The bicentenary of his birth marked a poignant occasion to reflect on his contested legacy, explore his centrality to the shaping of the Irish Nationalist memory of the Great Famine and revisit the debate concerning his contentious stance on slavery. Despite this, the President of Ireland, Michael D. Higgins, made reference to Mitchel in his speech at the 2016 Commemoration at Glasnevin cemetery, and the 2017 Commemoration will be held at Ballingarry, scene of the 1848 'famine rebellion', described by Mitchel as a 'poor extemporised *abortion of a rising*'.

It is now twenty years since the publication of *The Famine in Ulster*, edited by Christine Kinealy and Trevor Parkhill. This collection of nine essays offered a systematic survey of the impact of the Great Famine across the province's counties. That Ulster was found to have been 'affected severely' undoubtedly helped challenge the still widespread popular view that the northern province had uniformly escaped a crisis strongly associated with the rural west. Significant additional attention to the northern dimensions of the crisis emerged with the landmark publication of the *Atlas of the Great Irish Famine* in 2012. This work was an important statement about the wave of fresh research unleashed around 1995, the time of the 150th anniversary of the Great Famine's outbreak, after a long period of relative neglect. In its wake, it was increasingly difficult to offer neat generalisations about the crisis and readers became acutely aware that so much could differ between one locality and another, sometimes only miles apart.

In thinking about the Great Famine and its commemoration, one's thoughts are naturally drawn to the collection of essays eventually published in 1956 as *The Great Famine: Studies in Irish History, 1845–52*, under the editorship of Robert Dudley Edwards and Thomas Desmond Williams. Although the Famine certainly still loomed large in the popular consciousness of Ireland in the 1950s, the broader context was inevitably different from today. Larger numbers of citizens, north and south, have experienced more direct engagement, often at community level, with the crisis of the late 1840s. The editors of this volume were keen to try and reflect this public history participation here.

We hope that the work gathered here will add further to the debate about the historical geography of the crisis of the late 1840s. A number of shorter pieces have been included in Chapter 8, based on the Japanese rapid-fire presentation style, *pecha kucha*. These, it is hoped, will expand the range of perspectives offered and introduce fresh voices to the conversation. Whilst some of the authors are academic historians, others write from the vantage point of theology, family history, local history or museology. We hope these voices serve to enrich the collection.

Though not all of the essays focus explicitly on Ulster, the weight of the volume contributes meaningfully to what we might describe as Ulster Famine studies. Collectively, the authors perhaps shift the perspective away from a concentration upon the institutional history of the Crisis towards a range of dimensions which serve to break new ground. Looking at the experience of the late 1840s from the stance of those not always to the forefront of historical research is a welcome feature of the work, and revealing new or previously neglected evidence should encourage new questions and fresh enquiry. Given that population decline in the northern province during the Great Famine resulted disproportionately from the impact of emigration, as opposed to excess mortality or averted births, it is appropriate that several of these essays offer, in one way or another, a diasporic perspective. As Carlingford Lough represented the last sight of home for many who departed in these traumatic years, this represents a welcome feature and serves to connect Newry, its hinterland and its diaspora.

The impact of relief and capital remitted from migrants gone overseas is explored in a number of essays. Although in Ulster we remain prone to conceive of emigration as a pre-Famine phenomenon, we must acknowledge the massive acceleration in departures which occurred after 1845. The hundreds of thousands of emigrants from Ulster who went in half a decade established the momentum which allowed well over a million Ulster men and women to leave before the outbreak of the First World War. The true significance of the Famine exodus from the northern province has been somewhat obscured in the past. Let us hope that this collection can play some modest part in revising those perceptions.

Chapter One

The Women of Belfast and the Great Famine

Christine Kinealy

While the significance of the role of private charity in Ireland during the Famine is being increasingly acknowledged, the contribution that Irish people made in assisting other Irish people is largely unrecognised.[1] Moreover, the crucial role played by women in this process still remains mostly unknown.[2] This chapter explores the role played by two Belfast committees that were comprised of women, that is, the Ladies' Relief Association for Connaught and the Belfast Ladies' Association for the Relief of Irish Destitution.

Regardless of the outpouring of publications since 1995 relating to the Great Hunger, the role of Belfast and the north east of Ulster during periods of food shortages and hunger remains largely under-represented in famine historiography. A widespread assumption has been that, following the Act of Union, this part of the country fared better than other regions in Ireland due to more industrialisation, the widespread growth of oats, better security for tenants provided by the Ulster Custom, and the Protestantism of the majority of the population. A number of historians have suggested (erroneously) that the poor of the north coped better during the Great Famine, one suggesting: 'Ulster fared better than the average experience of the island … The Protestant people of that province suffered less severely from Famine'.[3] Belfast, however, like other major towns and cities, played a complex role, simultaneously being both a site of famine and a location for fundraising for the hungry. Women in the town of Belfast were to the forefront of negotiating this difficult situation, and they responded by establishing charitable organisations that provided relief, not only within Belfast itself, but to the rest of the country also.

In response to the deepening crisis in Ireland following the second failure of the potato crop, three relief bodies were established in the town: the Ladies' Relief Association for Connaught, which limited its efforts to the west of Ireland, the Belfast Ladies' Association and the Belfast General Relief Fund, both of which operated on an all-Ireland basis. The Belfast General Relief Fund had first convened on 2 January 1847, largely at the initiative of Dr John Edgar, the Presbyterian Moderator who was also closely associated with the Ladies' Relief Association for Connaught.[4] It was an exclusively male body that was associated with the main Protestant Churches, with Dr Thomas Drew, the Anglican Minister of Christ Church in College Square, also playing a leading role as Secretary of the Fund. Drew, an evangelical, was known for his anti-Catholic views, which increased sectarian tensions within the community.[5] The formation of the Belfast Ladies' Association and the Belfast General Relief Fund coincided with reports appearing in the local press of deaths from destitution in the town.[6] Consequently, the two committees decided that Belfast would not be excluded from receiving grants from them.[7] The local grants given by the General Relief Funds included £900 to support the work of the Soup Kitchen Committee, which provided relief at the quayside, mostly to paupers who had been returned from England and Scotland under their respective Laws of Settlement.[8] This is one example of the importance of private charity being able to intervene when the official channels of relief proved to be too bureaucratic and cumbersome to provide emergency, short-term relief.

Private charity did not exist in a hermetically sealed vacuum. Sectarian divisions, evangelical aspirations, political opportunism, attitudes to the poor and perceptions of gender roles, in varying degrees, shaped the ways in which relief was provided. Nevertheless, regardless of these and other challenges, Belfast women played an important role both as fundraisers and as givers of relief throughout the Famine of the late 1840s. Entrenched attitudes towards women participating in this public sphere of activity were apparent at the highest levels. Charles Trevelyan, Permanent Secretary at the British Treasury and overseer of all relief operations, informed one bank that was handling famine donations, 'as the persons who would avail themselves of this assistance are mostly ladies and clergymen and other persons not conversant with business, the notice should be of the plainest description, and give the direction of the office in London, and a list of the towns in Ireland in which your branch banks are situated'.[9] However, Trevelyan had underestimated the abilities of the women. As their activities in Belfast and elsewhere demonstrated, women were adept at forming committees, raising funds and distributing relief in a way that was practical, direct and often lifesaving.

The first ladies' association to be formed in Belfast was the Ladies' Relief Association for Connaught. The Association had been the idea of Dr John Edgar, Moderator of the Presbyterian Church of Ireland since 1842 and Secretary of the Assembly's Home Mission. When travelling in Connaught during the autumn of 1846 he had witnessed peoples' distress, realising that 'if relief do not come speedily, [hundreds] will in a few weeks die of hunger'.[10] He penned his concerns in a letter to the editor of the *Banner of Ulster*, from Killala in County Mayo, dated 13 September 1846, in which he affirmed: 'Private benevolence must awake at once, and give and work for those that are ready to perish'.[11]

Edgar's letter was reprinted in many other newspapers and circulated in Britain and Ireland, which resulted in his receiving a number of donations. Upon his return to Belfast, he made a direct entreaty to the local townspeople to provide continued assistance, but he turned to women to create a channel to ensure that these resources would reach those who needed them, which resulted in the formation of the Ladies' Relief Association for Connaught in October 1846.[12] The following month, Edgar's plea was reprinted by the Presbyterian Church as 'A Cry For Connaught—appeal for a land that fainteth by reason of a famine of bread and of hearing the words of the Lord'.[13] While his compassion for the poor in the west of Ireland was evident, Edgar's deeply held evangelical views and his longer-term desire to make converts was also apparent:

> I hope soon to have an opportunity of directing public attention to spiritual famine in Connaught, but our effort now is to save the perishing body and, whether our countryman and brother be a Protestant or Romanist, we acknowledge the claim which, in the day of his deep distress, he has on our purses and our hearts. Our brother is starving, and, till we have satisfied his hunger, we have no time to inquire whether he is Protestant or Romanist.[14]

The first women to become involved in the Association were drawn from congregations associated with the Rosemary Street Presbyterian Churches.[15] One of their first public fundraising activities was to hold a bazaar at which 'fancy ware' was sold. The holding of these bazaars had been used by the anti-slavery societies on both sides of the Atlantic, with women usually being the driving force behind them. The sales from the bazaar, together with other subscriptions received, raised £1,000.[16] Even after the bazaar was closed, the Association kept receiving contributions, resulting in the resumption of a more permanent bazaar in the Music Hall after 5 February.[17] Much of the work on sale had been donated from England and Scotland and was described as including a number of 'valuable paintings'.[18]

The early intervention of this society provided inspiration for other women to act. In November 1846, an anonymous appeal was made through a local newspaper to the 'Ladies of Tralee'. Government relief in the town was proving inadequate in providing either work or relief to the local poor and although the local gentry had raised £900, this money had been quickly used. To raise more funds, the anonymous author of the letter suggested that the local ladies have a sale of their needlework in the period before Christmas. The involvement of women in the north was held up as an example:

> There was a sale of Ladies' work within the last two months in Cookstown, a small town in west Ulster, containing some 2,000 inhabitants, which produced £250. The overwhelming destitution of Connemara at the present crisis, as detailed by an eye witness, has awakened the sympathy and united the efforts of the Ladies of Belfast in its behalf. A work association has been formed, and an agent employed to visit the towns and villages of Ulster, to organize branch associations, and it is confidently anticipated that many hundreds of pounds will be realized by the effort before Christmas.
>
> Now, what these benevolent females are doing for the poor and destitute of another province, I humbly suggest to the Ladies of Tralee might be done by them for the poor and destitute of their own town.[19]

In addition to the sale of work, the Ladies' Relief Association received donations, many from Britain, but also from a number of Irish landowners, including Lord Roden and Lord Lurgan.[20] They included donations from other women's organisations that had been formed in response to the Famine in Ireland, such as the Edinburgh Ladies' Association who sent the sum of £50 to the treasurer of the Belfast Ladies' Association in April.[21] Some months later the Edinburgh Association, which had been formed in response to Dr Edgar's appeal, raised a large sum of money to pay for Revd Robert Allen to establish a 'mission' in Connaught.[22]

William Bennett, an English Quaker who visited Ireland in the spring of 1847 for the purpose of distributing seed to the poor, observed the impact of the Association's work first hand, both in Belfast and when travelling in the west. In an account of his time in Ireland, Bennett included a number of letters written to the 'Connaught Committee' which provided an insight into how the money was being used, in this case, to set up a loom in a clergyman's stable. The money used in this instance had been sent by a ladies' committee in London to the Belfast women:

> The following is the acknowledgment addressed to one of the active ladies of the Connaught Committee … 'Castlebar, Mayo, April 2nd, 1847. I received your letter of the 30th of March, enclosing £5, for re-productive works of industry, for which I am very thankful. I am happy to say the object in view is going on very favourably, as far as the money at our disposal enables us to work. My daughters have sixty poor females employed, and I have as many spinning and weaving. They are preparing articles for the public sale in Dublin. We have labour cheap; all we want is skill, energy, and a little capital to set us going. I hope, if the Lord will, to live to see the day, when Mayo will be like the North of Ireland. Prices of food are coming down, but alas! the land lies waste, – little or no tillage, no seeds.' Again, under date April 7th. 'We got a woman to instruct our girls in knitting and spinning. Enclosed is a specimen stocking, which appears very soft and good. Such would be made to order at one shilling a pair, we finding all materials. I also send two specimens from the looms I am setting to work. They are good; the next pieces will be better I hope, these are the first.' Enclosed were the specimens, with size and price, and labelled as 'made by poor starving persons in Mayo, in a loom set up in the clergyman's stable.'[23]

By the end of 1847, the Ladies' Relief Association had raised £4,615 6s 1d.[24] Virtually all of this money had been used to distribute gratuitous relief to the destitute, with no labour or reading of Bibles required in return. At this stage, Edgar decided that the work of the committee would be more useful if they focused on teaching the poor in Connaught how to earn their own income.[25] Subsequent donations, therefore, were to be used to establish 'industrial schools' in which the children would be taught needlework and knitting. While the children worked, they were also taught to read 'and made familiar with the Scriptures'.[26] If they could not attend school, they were encouraged to read the Bible at home.[27] This marked a significant change in the purpose of the Society in moving it closer to the proselytising efforts of other Protestant Missions. Asenath Nicholson, an American who visited some of the Industrial schools in Connaught, praised the idea of promoting industry and self-help amongst the poor, believing that as a consequence 'an industry, founded on righteous principles, was springing up – an industry that not only rewarded but elevated – the convenient term "lazy Irish", was hiding its slanderous head'.[28] The work of the Society was also admired by the Society of Friends who gave it a grant of £500 in May 1848.[29] A condition of this grant was that an equal amount should be raised from other sources.[30] The work of the Ladies' Industrial Association continued after the country began to recover from the Famine.[31] At the beginning of 1851, Dr Edgar had fifty-six female teachers working with 2,000 pupils and their families.[32]

The Belfast Ladies' Association for the Relief of Irish Destitution was formed on 1 January 1847. The origins of the Association lay in adverts that appeared in a number of local newspapers inviting 'ladies of all Christian sects' to attend a meeting, 'in order to provide relief for the distressed without regard to denominational distinctions'.[33] The first meeting of the Association was described as 'a large and influential assemblage of Ladies of all religious denominations'. It took place in the Commercial Buildings, but following this, weekly meetings were held on Saturdays in the Library of the Royal Belfast Academical Institution.[34] The inaugural meeting was presided over by 'Miss Knowles',[35] who also made a donation of £50.[36] Fanny Knowles, who owned a day school for ladies, was the sister of the dramatist and actor, James Sheridan Knowles.[37]

The committee was professionally organised, with a number of sub-committees being established, which included Corresponding, Clothing, Industrial, Collecting and Bazaar Committees.[38] To raise funds, Belfast was divided into a number of districts and subscription lists were opened in each of them. In the spring, a Bazaar was planned to augment these funds. Donations were also sought from Scotland and England. The Association's early commitment to 'sink all doctrinal distinctions' and provide assistance without regard to religion was praised by Nicholson, who, like Bennett, observed their work first hand.[39]

The Belfast Association consisted of 115 members, with Miss Knowles as President. Isabella Campbell Allen, wife of the wealthy Unitarian merchant, William Campbell Allen, was Treasurer of the Industrial Committee, which financed and sold locally made linen and knitwear.[40] The Treasurers were Mrs J. Andrews of 60 Donegall Street,[41] Mrs J.S. Porter of 16 College Square[42] and Mrs J.T. Tennent of Hazelbank.[43] The Secretaries were Mrs D.L. Boyd of 7 Chichester Street, Miss Murney of 18 High Street[44] and Miss McDowell of 35 Arthur Street.[45] One of the most well-known members was Mary Ann McCracken, then aged seventy-seven, and a noted social reformer and philanthropist.[46] She was sister to Henry Joy McCracken, who had been executed in 1798 for his part in the rebellion. Even in old age, Mary Ann shared many of his egalitarian ideals, including a commitment to the abolition of slavery.[47] Maria Webb, a fellow abolitionist and a Quaker, was one of the founding members of the Ladies' Association. She was also Secretary of the Belfast Ladies Anti-Slavery Society.[48] Within the United States, she and her family were well known in anti-slavery circles, their friends including Frederick Douglass. In January 1847, Webb wrote a letter to her American colleagues, which was published in a number of newspapers. She explained:

> I have been, for the last few weeks, overpowered with business arising out of the arrangements on behalf of the famishing, destitute, state of our own peasantry. I do not mean the peasantry in districts surrounding Belfast, but distant agricultural counties, where things are truly in an awful state … Can America do anything to save our poor people from utter starvation?[49]

In December 1847, Webb contacted Maria Weston Chapman in Boston on behalf of the Belfast Ladies' Anti-Slavery Committee. For a number of years, Irish women abolitionists had been sending locally made products to be sold at the Boston Anti-Slavery Bazaar. In that year, however, she apologised for the smallness of the offering, explaining that the Belfast women had been preoccupied in looking after the poor within Ireland.[50] Other members of the Ladies' Association included Mary Ireland who, like Webb and McCracken, was a prominent member of the local anti-slavery movement and therefore accustomed to committee work.[51]

The approach to fundraising by the two ladies' associations was similar. An early decision made by the Ladies' Relief Association was to hold an Easter fundraising bazaar to assist those 'who are held down by the heavy hand of famine'.[52] They also organised for subscriptions to be raised throughout, an action that very much brought them into the public sphere. Like the other charitable organisations they received a number of donations from individuals, one of the most unusual coming from the actor

J. Vandenhoff, who gave £76, the proceedings of a reading of *Hamlet*, which he had performed in Belfast.[53]

By early March, the Belfast Ladies' Association had raised over £2,000 in monetary aid.[54] They decided to use these resources, in the first instance, to assist mothers and their families who were in the greatest need.[55] Aid was provided initially in the form of cash and clothing, the former for the purpose of purchasing food and fuel, the latter being especially crucial in such a cold winter. Clothing was essential, especially for those employed on the public works in freezing, snowy conditions. Large supplies of clothing and clothing materials were given to the Belfast Ladies' Association from England, coming from towns and cities as far apart as Newcastle upon Tyne and Worcester. The largest individual donation of clothing came from Carlisle, in the far north of England, where a 'Ladies' Association for the Irish Poor' had been formed. They contributed 1,372 articles.[56]

Within weeks of being established, the Ladies' Association was handing out substantial grants to a variety of locations, as demonstrated by their Minutes of 13 February:

> £100, with five pound's worth of clothing, to the Belfast local committee; five pound's worth of clothing, to the Rev. Ed. Le Batt, Killgar, county Donegal; ten pound's worth of clothing, to the Rev. William Baillie, Fanet Glebe, Ramelton, county Donegal; five pound's worth of clothing, to the Rev. Simon Foote, Glenadry, Portadown; £10, with twenty pound's worth of clothing, to Mrs. Griffith, Templecrone, county Donegal; fifteen pound's worth of clothing, to Mrs. Knox, Donamon, county Roscommon; twenty pound's worth of clothing, to Mrs. Holmes, Clogher, county Mayo; twenty pound's worth of clothing, to the Rev. B. Smith, Cornwall, county Donegal; £20, placed at the disposal of the industrial committee for the employment of the poor females of the parish of Cornwall; and five pound's worth of clothing to Mrs. Burley, Tullydeagh, Enniskillen.[57]

A week later, more grants were distributed:

> £100 to the treasurer of the industrial committee. £10, with £3 worth of clothing to each of the relief committees of Kilmore and Mullavilla, two divisions of the parish of Kilmore, county Armagh. £20 worth of clothing, with £10 for food, and £10 for the industrial occupation

of the poor females of the parish, to the Rev. J. Thompson, Raphoe, Donegal. £10 to the Rev. P. Sullivan, Mayo, Ballyglass, county Mayo; for the industrial occupation of the poor females of his parish. £10 to Mr. Tracer, Loobvenoy, Scariff. £6 worth of clothing to Mrs. Elliott, Smythborough. The following grants were made during the past week, by the industrial committee: — £10 to the 'Ladies' Relief Association,' Ballyshannon, per Miss Allingham. £20 to the Rev. William Baillie, Fermet Glebe, Ramelton. £15 to Wybrants Olphert, Esq., Ballyconnell house, Dunfanaghy. £20 to the Rev. Patrick Leaghy, the College, Thurles, Tipperary. £10 to the Rev. Thomas Thompson, Deriaghy, Lisburn.[58]

On 6 March, the following grants were made:

£10 to Mr. John Minnows, secretary of the relief committee, Tempe, Roscommon. £10 to Mr. Nicholas Kelly, secretary of the relief committee, Craggs, Athleague, Roscommon. £10 to Mr. Thos. Kelly, secretary of the relief committee, Ballinoe, county Galway. £100 to the treasurer of the industrial committee, to enable that committee to make such grants for industrial purposes as they find most expedient. £50 to the treasurer of the clothing committee, for the purchase of material, and to pay for the making up of clothing for the poor. £20, through Miss Archer, to the relief committee of Dingle. £20 to Mr. Sufficld, secretary to the relief committee, Clifton, Connemara. £20 worth of clothing to the Rev. Hugh Hamilton, treasurer of the relief committee, Benmore, county Fermanagh. £10 worth of clothing, through Mrs. Maturin, Garton Glebe, Letterkenny, county Donegal, to the relief committee of that parish. £10, through Mrs. Birkehoffer, Ballybournie, Macroom, county Cork, to the Rev. P. Houstan, secretary for the relief committee of that parish. £10, with £10 worth of clothing, to Mr. Davison, Dromonrne, Glenarms. £10 to the Rev. George Ashe, for distribution in his parish.[59]

An insight into the impact of the distribution of clothing was provided by Captain Jones, an agent of the British Relief Association who was based in Donegal. He reported that the people of Arranmore Island were 'the best clothed people I have ever met,' which he attributed to a 'liberal contribution' from the Ladies' Society of Belfast and the Society of Friends. However, they were also starving. Jones lamented that although the island was surrounded by plentiful numbers of fish – cod, ling and turbot – the people had no fishing tackle. Before leaving the island, he provided £10 for the purchase of fishing tackle, which was then sold locally at a reduced rate.[60] His action provided a further example of the ability of private charity to respond to local needs as they arose.

Regardless of the success of their early interventions, after only two months in operation the Belfast Ladies' Association decided to use their funds to support 'industrial pursuits', as a way of eking out their limited resources and helping to preserve a spirit of independence amongst the recipients. Moreover, they saw this shift of emphasis as the best way of helping to 'preserve the females from the moral evils which have sometimes arisen from their engaging in company with promiscuous assemblages of persons of the other sex, as labourers on the road or other public works'.[61] They hoped that larger charitable organisations would continue to provide food in these districts. Instead, the Ladies' Association now focused on providing grants, often to be used to purchase flax for spinning or yarn for knitting.[62]

Although the Belfast Ladies' Association provided assistance to all parts of the country, the majority of the demands made on their charity came from counties Antrim and Donegal in Ulster, and from County Mayo in Connacht. One aspect of their work that surprised the women was the deteriorating conditions in Belfast and the increasing demands made on them from the poor of the town. On 8 February, a number of women from the committee met at Blain's (possibly Dr Blain's Academy on Arthur Street) to consider, 'the best and most efficient means of relieving the distress now prevailing in the town of Belfast'.[63] While acknowledging the local suffering, the Association decided to continue to provide general relief, but some of their members had assisted with establishing a separate society for the poor of Belfast.[64]

From the outset, the Association had encouraged women in the most distressed districts to form their own associations and a number of requests were received from women both as individuals and on behalf of local associations. The latter included the newly formed ladies' associations of Killala and Newcastle, in counties Mayo and Limerick respectively.[65] Many appeals for aid were also made by Catholic priests and Anglican ministers to the Belfast Ladies' Association. Wives of Anglican ministers proved particularly active in distributing relief and providing employment on behalf of relief committees.[66] However, other women with no direct relationship to the churches proved to be energetic in helping the local poor. On 18 February, a Mrs Hewitson from Rossgarrow, near Milford in County Donegal, wrote that she and her daughters, together with some local women, had formed an Industrial Committee, of which she was both Treasurer and Secretary. For some weeks past they had been providing employment and food to local women, helped by small grants from the First and Second Unitarian Congregations of Belfast and by the Society of Friends. That money was now exhausted. The Belfast Ladies' Association had already sent them one consignment of clothing, which had arrived at the same time as 'a bitter snow storm'. Mrs Hewitson appealed for another batch to be sent, explaining:

> The children, in particular, are never half covered, and their few things seldom made to fit ... Some men are now working on the roads in thin linen jackets; and many starving beings, male and female, some of tender age, are now expecting employment on them, and anxiously imploring a covering from the exposure they are subject to, at such work.[67]

Asenath Nicholson, who had stayed with the Hewitson family while touring Ireland in 1847, praised them highly. She recorded that Mrs Hewitson rose at 4.00 am every morning to make food for the local poor, who, 'through the day made the habitation a nucleus not of the most pleasant kind. The lower window frame in the kitchen was of board instead of glass, this all having been broken by the pressure of faces continually there'.[68] Nicholson, who was an eyewitness to so much misery, admitted that her 'heart was tortured with unparalleled scenes of suffering'.[69]

Similar levels of distress were apparent in other appeals directed at the Belfast women. An application was made to the Belfast Ladies' Association by the resident ministers in Templecrone in Dungloe, County Donegal. They had visited the island of Arranmore and were shocked by what they saw. Their request ended on a sombre note:

> In since calmly reviewing and reflecting upon the harrowing and revolting incidents that were crowded into our hurried walk, through but a part of the island, and that on a short Winter's day, we feel astonished and dismayed at the accumulating misery that presented itself to us; and we mourn, as we feel persuaded that such afflictions are but the shadows of things to come, and the beginning of unutterable horrors.[70]

The Belfast Committee responded by sending 'a noble donation' of £60 for the islanders, and £5 for the parish in general.[71]

Again, the agency of women was evident from the submissions made to the Association. Mrs Hume, from Glen Lodge in Killybegs, wanted to establish a knitting group for local women, asking the Belfast Ladies' Association to provide a grant for this purpose.[72] Her correspondence with the Belfast women demonstrated her frustrations with the limitations of government relief measures:

> The aid, which has been obtained, by Government employing some on the public works, is very inadequate to the extent of want. The limitations of one only being employed out of a very large family, at 9d a day affords to a laboring man, with six or eight children, a scanty pittance for their support. The females are totally unemployed, in a state of wretchedness and want, and would require some active efforts to relieve them by giving work.

A few weeks later, William Hume JP, of the same address, wrote a frustrated letter to the Relief Commission in Dublin, which he concluded by saying:

> I must confess, as a Landlord (not receiving any rent) my inability to assist my poor tenants in their need. But the plan of the Commissary General, I suppose, accords with the views of Government, to procrastinate relief, until starvation and death ensues. This is, I assure you, the general impression.[73]

These letters, outlining dissatisfaction with government relief, reinforced the importance of groups such as the Belfast Ladies' Association. Mrs Hume was awarded a grant of £10 by the Belfast committee, she promising to 'expend it judiciously, so as to cultivate a love for feminine habits of industry amongst our females, who have hitherto known and understood only working in the fields'.[74]

In total, the Belfast Ladies' Association raised £2,617 1s 6d.[75] Like many other charitable organisations, they experienced a drying up of donations at the end of 1847. Many of the women involved in this organisation later turned their energies and abilities to supporting an Industrial School in

Belfast, which they opened in Frederick Street in November 1847. Most of those who attended were aged under twelve, and were employed in manufacturing 'English lace'.[76] The women who managed it used the same system of fundraising and organisation that had proved so effective to the Belfast Ladies' Association.[77] The school's female origins were made evident by the fact that it continued to be referred to as the 'Ladies' Industrial School'.[78]

The hard work and inclusive approach of these women won the praise of Nicholson, who had the opportunity to meet with many ladies' associations as she travelled throughout the country. She was unequivocal in her approval, writing: 'The Belfast Ladies' Association embraces an object which lives and tells, and will continue to do so, when they who formed it shall be no longer be on earth'.[79] Though Nicholson was impressed with the two ladies' committees in Belfast, she was less flattering regarding the ladies' committees that had been formed in Dublin. While the latter were effective in raising money, Nicholson believed that they were less diligent in providing relief, suggesting that, 'giving and doing are antipodes in her who has never been trained to domestic duties'.[80]

The Belfast women won the praise of other visitors to Ireland, including William Bennett, whose own sister was a member of the Quaker Ladies' Committee in London, which had been established to send clothing and blankets to Ireland. He observed the Belfast committees first hand:

> I must not omit to mention here the great kindness we received from the members of both the Ladies' Associations of Belfast. The older one, especially for 'Connaught,' originated in the exertions of Dr. Edgar, one of the first to awaken public attention and sympathy to the threatening calamity, and the real condition of the Western peasantry ... It was presumed the extremities of neglect and destitution were nearly confined to Connaught; and no conception was then entertained, that it would extend equally into other districts, and, as it were, over-spread the land. This called up the second Ladies' Association, with a wider sphere. Both have been most active and zealous; and both have had their successful bazaars. Both also have looked beyond the present emergency; and propose rendering themselves permanent for educational and industrial objects, and are worthy of the best support ... their active and enterprising spirit will not be readily laid.[81]

Bennett also noted that the work of these committees was being carried out against a backdrop of increasing distress within Belfast, making their activities even more challenging.

The two women's organisations were also praised in local newspapers. The Belfast Ladies' Association was given special recognition for providing relief 'without regard to place or persuasion'. It added:

> We do not recapitulate these great efforts in any spirit of boasting, though we are naturally proud that our town should be the theatre of them; but we should think that we departed from our duty, as public journalists, if we did not encourage such movements with the echo of our praise, and hold them up as an example to other communities to 'go and do likewise.'

Less charitably perhaps, and inserting a political note into the discussion, the newspaper concluded by stating: 'What a favourable contrast does Belfast present, at this moment, to other towns in Ireland', and pointing out that while the town of Wexford was doing little to assist its poor, it was sending large amounts to the Repeal cause in Dublin.[82]

Inevitably, charity was subject to the same value codes that dictated attitudes towards the poor in the mid-nineteenth century, based on blaming the poor for their own poverty, a fear of creating a culture of dependency, the drawing of a distinction between 'deserving' and 'undeserving' poor, and seeking to use charity as a tool of moral rehabilitation, and, in regard to Ireland, of national regeneration. However, for a short period, religious and other differences were put to one side as the women of Belfast worked to alleviate the hunger and other needs of their fellow Irish men and women in an efficient and effective manner. In the longer term, as the work of the ladies' committees evolved, sectarian differences and proselytising objectives again reared their ugly heads. This did not diminish the value of the intervention of the women of Belfast in providing relief during 1847. They lived up to the maxim that charity did begin at home.

Notes

1 An exception is the role of the Quakers in Ireland. See R. Goodbody, *A Suitable Channel: Quaker Relief in the Great Famine* (Dublin: Pale Publications, 1995) and C. Kinealy, *Charity and the Great Hunger: The Kindness of Strangers* (London: Bloomsbury, 2013).

2 See C. Kinealy et al., *Women and the Great Hunger* (Quinnipiac, Conn.: Quinnipiac University Press and Cork University Press, 2016).
3 L. Kennedy, 'The Rural Economy' in L. Kennedy and P. Ollerenshaw, *An Economic History of Ulster* (Manchester: Manchester University Press, 1985), p. 30.
4 'Destitution', *Belfast News Letter*, 5 January 1849.
5 In 1857, Drew's virulently anti-Catholic sermon given to local Orangemen is thought to have led to two months of sectarian rioting. See H. McLeod, *European Religion in the Age of Great Cities: 1830–1930* (London: Routledge, 2005), p. 151.
6 'Destitution', *Belfast News Letter*, 5 January 1847.
7 'Belfast General Relief Fund', *Belfast News Letter*, 12 February 1847.
8 'Belfast General Relief Fund', *Belfast News Letter*, 5 January 1849.
9 Trevelyan to Mr Hewat, Provincial Bank, 1 March 1847, *House of Commons Papers* (London: House of Commons), vol. 52, p. 213.
10 'Famine in Connaught', reprinted in W.D. Killen, *Memoir of Dr John Edgar* (Belfast: C. Aitchison, 1867), p. 203.
11 Ibid. p. 207.
12 W.D. Killen, *The Ecclesiastical History of Ireland: From the Earliest Period to the Present Times*, vol. 2 (London: Macmillan, 1875), p. 496.
13 'A Cry from Connaught' was printed in the *Missionary Herald* of November 1846.
14 Killen, 'Appeal in Belfast', *Ecclesiastical History*, vol. 2, pp. 217–18.
15 The first Presbyterian Church on Rosemary Street was also at this time referred to as the First Unitarian Church of Belfast.
16 'Public Benevolence of Belfast', *Belfast News Letter*, 5 January 1847.
17 'Ladies Bazaar', ibid., 5 January 1847.
18 'This Day', 'Ladies Bazaar', ibid.
19 'To the Ladies of Tralee', *Kerry Evening Post*, 11 November 1846. The letter was signed by 'A Friend of the Poor'.
20 Dr J. Edgar, *Connaught – Spiritual and Temporal – The Cry Heard* (Belfast: Banner of Ulster Office, 1847).
21 'Belfast Relief Association', *Nation*, 8 May 1847.
22 Killen, *Memoir*, p. 251.
23 W. Bennett, *Narrative of a Recent Journey of Six Weeks in Ireland* (London: C. Gilpin, 1847), pp. 91–2.
24 The Society of Friends, *Transactions of the Central Relief Committee of the Society of Friends During the Famine in Ireland, in 1846 and 1847* (Dublin: Hodges and Smith, 1852), p. 46.
25 Ibid. Statement Dr Edgar of Belfast, p. 436.
26 Killen, *Ecclesiastical History*, vol. 2, p. 496.
27 Ibid.
28 A. Nicholson, *Annals of the Famine in Ireland, in 1847, 1848, and 1849* (New York: E. French, 1851), p. 59.
29 Minutes of Central Relief Committee, 25 May 1848, *Transactions*, p. 436.
30 Ibid. p. 92.
31 J. Edgar, *The Women of the West: Ireland Helped to Help Herself* (Belfast: Banner of Ulster Office, 1849).
32 Shaftesbury Society and Ragged School Union, *The Ragged School Union Magazine*, vol. 5 (London: Partridge and Oakey, 1853), p. 190.
33 'Meeting of Ladies', *Belfast News Letter*, 5 January 1847.

34 *First Report of Belfast Ladies' Committee* [hereafter, *Report of BLC*], 6 March 1847 (Belfast: 1847), p. 1.
35 Miss Fanny Knowles ran a boarding and day school at 30 Upper Arthur Street in Belfast.
36 'Meeting of Ladies', *Belfast News Letter*, 5 January 1847.
37 James Sheridan Knowles dedicated his work, *The Elocutionist* (1854), to his sister, Fanny.
38 *Report of BLC*, pp. 4–5.
39 Nicholson, *Annals*, pp. 58–60.
40 Public Record Office of Northern Ireland [hereafter, PRONI], D1558/7/1/. Campbell Allen Papers: https://www.nidirect.gov.uk/sites/default/files/publications/campbell-allen-d1558.pdf (accessed 5 May 2017).
41 Wife of James Andrews, a solicitor. Finding information on these women is difficult, especially as the married women identify by using their husbands' names.
42 Margaret Porter was wife of Revd J. Scott Porter, a minister in Rosemary Street First Presbyterian Church.
43 Wife of James Thompson Tennent, a magistrate and Director of the Ulster Banking Company.
44 Daughter of Henry Murney, a wine and tea merchant and tobacco manufacturer.
45 'Belfast Ladies Association', *Belfast News Letter*, 29 January 1847.
46 M. McNeill, *The Life and Times of Mary Ann McCracken, 1770–1866: A Belfast Panorama* (Dublin: A. Figgis, 1960).
47 C. Kinealy, *Daniel O'Connell and the Anti-Slavery Movement: The Saddest People the Sun Sees* (London: Pickering and Chatto, 2011).
48 S. Rhoads and E. Lewis, *Friends' Review: A Religious, Literary and Miscellaneous Journal*, vol. 27 (Philadelphia: J. Tatum, 1875), p. 747.
49 *National Era*, 4 February 1847.
50 Maria Webb to Maria Weston Chapman, 2 December 1847, Boston Library digitised anti-slavery collection: http://archive.org/details/lettertomariacha00webb (accessed 10 October 2016).
51 Nicholson, *Annals*, p. 60; Kinealy, *Daniel O'Connell and the Anti-Slavery Movement.*
52 'Belfast Ladies' Association', *Belfast News Letter*, 29 January 1847.
53 T. Marshall, *Lives of the most Celebrated Actors and Actresses, etc.* (London: E. Appleyard, 1848?).
54 *Report of BLC*, pp. 2–10.
55 Ibid.
56 Ibid. Report of Clothing Committee, p. 36.
57 'Belfast Ladies' Association for Belfast', *Belfast News Letter*, 19 February 1847.
58 'Belfast Ladies' Association for the Relief of Irish Distress', *Belfast News Letter*, 26 March 1847.
59 Ibid. (untitled), 12 March 1847.
60 Capt. Jones, Letterkenny, 22 May 1847, *Report of British Relief Association for the Relief of Distress in Ireland and the Highlands of Scotland* (London: Richard Clay, 1849), p. 120.
61 *Report of BLC*, pp. 10–20.
62 Ibid. Report of Operations of Industrial Committee', pp. 27–30.
63 'Belfast Ladies' Association', *Belfast News Letter*, 12 February 1847.
64 *Report of BLC*, pp. 7–8. See also, C. Kinealy and G. Mac Atasney, *The Hidden Famine: Hunger, Poverty and Sectarianism in Belfast* (London: Pluto Press, 2000).
65 *Report of BLC*, p. 28.

66 Ibid. pp. 20–30.
67 Ibid. Mrs Hewitson, Rossgarrow (incorrectly printed as Rossgarron), 18 February 1847, pp. 17–19.
68 Nicholson, *Annals*, p. 82.
69 Ibid. p. 83.
70 *Report of BLC*, Revd P. Griffiths and Dr Brady, Templecrone, p. 25.
71 Ibid. Revd Griffiths to Ladies' Committee, 4 February 1847, p. 25.
72 Ibid. Mrs Hume, Glen Lodge Killibegs, 3 February 1847, p. 33.
73 National Archive of Ireland (NAI), RLFC 3/2/7/8. Relief Commission Papers, William Hume to William Stanley Esquire, 2 April 1847: www.learnaboutarchives.ie/~learnabo/images/learnaboutarchives/sampledocuments/famine/donegaltranscript1.pdf (accessed 1 May 2016).
74 Ibid. 22 February 1847. William Hume, who was a JP, died in November 1849: *Headstone Inscriptions,* St *Columba's Church of Ireland, Glencolumbkille*: http://donegalgenealogy.com/stccofi.htm (accessed 5 May 2017).
75 *Transactions*, p. 46.
76 J. Sproule (ed.), *The Resources and Manufacturing Industry of Ireland: As Illustrated by the Exhibition of 1853* (Dublin: John Sproule, 1854), p. 338.
77 'Bazaar', *Belfast News Letter*, 9 January 1849.
78 W. McComb, *Guide to Belfast: The Giant's Causeway, and the Adjoining Districts of the Antrim and Down* (Belfast: W. McComb, 1861), p. 28.
79 Nicholson, *Annals*, pp. 72–3.
80 Ibid. p. 57.
81 Bennett, *Narrative*, pp. 91–2.
82 'Public benevolence of Belfast', *Belfast News Letter,* 5 January 1847.

Chapter Two

The Demography of the Famine in Ulster: A Few Unanswered Questions, A Few New Sources[1]

Cormac Ó Gráda

At what level of aggregation should the Famine be analysed? Some data are available only at a fairly aggregated level, while a small number are available down to the urban level. Comparative analysis involves trade-offs between the level of aggregation and the choice of explanatory variables. While an artificial unit of analysis, the province, does have the charm of dividing the island into north, south, east and west, Ulster escaped the Famine more lightly than the other three provinces. But its impact, as reflected in population change between 1841 and 1851, was more uneven in Ulster than in any of the other three provinces. At county level, the border counties of Cavan, Fermanagh and Monaghan, where the population decline in many parishes exceeded one-third, were the worst hit. In this sense, the Famine was 'lightest' in west Donegal, in central Antrim, in the Lagan valley, by the southern shores of Lough Neagh and in north County Down. Only three of Ireland's 130 poor law unions deemed it unnecessary to distribute soup rations under the provisions of the Temporary Relief Act of 1847, and all three – Antrim, Belfast and Newtownards – were located in the industrialised east of the province.[2] Two recent maps capture these contrasts in fine detail: that in John Crowley et al.'s indispensable *Atlas of the Great Irish Famine*[3] – which, it should be noted, refers to the rural population of civil parishes – and that in the study by Fotheringham et al.,[4] which uses the district electoral division (DED) rather than the parish as the unit of analysis.[5]

In a small number of Ulster parishes the population rose between 1841 and 1851. They include the civil parishes of Newtown Crommelin in mid-Antrim (where the population rose from 799 in 1841 to 876 in 1851; Poor Law Valuation (PLV) £795 10s 0d), the Grange of Doagh in south Antrim (from 974 to 1,117; PLV £3,215) and Ardquin near the southern tip of the Ards Pensinula (from 916 to 918; PLV £3,344 5s 0d). The last two had relatively high PLVs per head – a convenient, rough-and-ready proxy for living standards. Newtown Crommelin escaped lightly for such a poor and heavily agricultural parish; perhaps less dependence on the potato played a part. But all three parishes are too small for province- or island-wide inferences. Templecorran in south-east Antrim (from 1,423 to 1,472; PLV £3,891) was also relatively well off, while the County Down parish of Tullylish (from 12,660 to 13,400; PLV £15,047) was shielded by its linen industry.[6]

But what of the Montiaghs on the shores of Lough Neagh (from 3,480 to 3,581; PLV £3,653) and of Killybegs Lower in south-west Donegal (from 3,290 to 3,338; PLV £1,560)? The data extracted from rentals, parish registers and workhouse records by the Lurgan historian F.X. McCorry[7] 'reflect well on the capability of the Montiagh's population to survive the Famine's chill', and he highlights the importance of the turf-cutting industry ('the supplier of turf to large portions of counties Armagh and Down') and domestic weaving as factors in keeping deaths down. McCorry also shows that while few entered the workhouse from the Montiaghs in 1847, when mortality was high, admissions were higher thereafter when deaths were fewer; an interesting finding which he interprets as evidence that 'few were sent to the workhouse to die during the Famine'. The Catholic parish of Seagoe includes the Montiaghs, and its parish records, which unusually also list burials, have been insightfully analysed by McCorry,[8] who finds that while mortality among Catholics in the Montiaghs was four times the pre-Famine average in 1847, peaking in March and April of that year, it was back to normal in the following year. As for the relatively low demographic toll in west and south-west Donegal, Breandán Mac Suibhne[9] has attributed that to heavy reliance on seasonal migration to Scotland, knitting, and sprigging, and the credit networks that those activities spawned.

Using Data on Baptisms

The Famine impacted on population in three ways: through excess mortality, through missing births and through emigration. Given the quality of the data, it is impossible to be precise about which of these factors mattered

Table 1. Annual excess mortality per 1,000 population, 1846–51: Ulster counties

County	Upper Bound	Lower Bound	County	Upper Bound	Lower Bound
Antrim	20.3	15.0	Down	12.5	6.7
Armagh	22.2	15.3	Fermanagh	39.1	29.2
Cavan	51.8	42.7	Monaghan	36.0	28.6
Derry	10.1	5.7	Tyrone	22.3	15.2
Donegal	18.7	10.7	Ulster	25.6	18.9
Leinster	14.2	8.9	Munster	36.3	24.9
Connacht	61.7	50.9	IRELAND	33.1	24.4

J. Mokyr, *Why Ireland Starved*, 2nd edition (London: Allen & Unwin, 1985), pp. 266–7.

most by county or by parish. The most reliable county estimates of excess mortality are those by Mokyr (see Table 1). His upper bound estimates represent 'the demographic deficit caused by the famine', whereas his lower bound estimates refer to excess mortality. The gap between them is a measure of 'averted births'. The county estimates of excess mortality depend on assumptions about emigration during the Famine, on which records are lacking. While Mokyr candidly admits that his procedures are 'very approximate', he reassures us with the claim that 'most of the results do not seem very sensitive to the assumptions employed'.[10]

A reduction in fertility is as much a hallmark of famine as an increase in deaths. While such a reduction might occasionally be planned or precautionary – as apparently happened in the western Netherlands during the *Hongerwinter* of 1944–5 – in general it is the product of spousal separation, reduced libido or, especially, famine amenorrhoea.[11] Where parish registers lack data on burials, the Italian historian Guido Alfani[12] has made a strong case for working with parish birth records as a sensitive measure of a famine's severity. In Ireland, many Roman Catholic parish registers from the Famine era have been available online since mid-2015;[13] some, such as that for Seagoe, contain data on burials as well as baptisms, but most record only the latter. Systematic analyses of a sample of these data should in time give us a good sense of the extent and variation in lost births during the 1840s. Alas, the survival of registers for the Famine years is patchy: nothing survives, for example, for west Donegal, an area of particular interest in this respect.[14] But where they do survive there is a presumption that they are reasonably complete, given the important role of baptism in the Catholic faith.

For the purposes of this chapter, we extracted data for the Catholic parishes listed in Table 2. We also report on Taughboyne and Derrylorn, two of the small number of Church of Ireland parishes whose records have been digitised.[15] For comparative perspective, we compare the outcome in Ulster

Table 2. Some details on the parishes described in the text

Parish	Location	Denomination	Pop. 1841	Pop. 1851	Poor Law Valuation (£)
Errigal Trough	Monaghan/ Tyrone	RC	9,585	7,171	12,004
Ballyphillip and Portaferry	Down	RC	3,086	2,833	5,013
Tydavnet	Monaghan	RC	11,645	8,442	14,755
Ramoan	North Antrim	RC	4,807	4,102	7,545
Desertcreight	Derry–Tyrone	RC			
Seagoe	North Armagh	RC	11,004	10,503	11,267
Clonfeacle	Tyrone	RC	18,930	13,810	26,010
Taughboyne	St Johnstone, Donegal	C of I	5,782	4,851	9,745
Derrylorn	Derry–Tyrone	C of I	8,480	7,552	13,103
Kenmare	South Kerry	RC	5,839	7,495	3,597
Tuosist	South Kerry	RC	7,485	4,034	2,472
Eyeries	South Kerry	RC			

Note: Kenmare workhouse held 3,353 inmates in 1851.

with that in three badly affected parishes in south Kerry: Kenmare, Tuosist and Eyeries.

The quarter-to-quarter variations in baptisms in these parishes between (when available) *c.*1840 and 1852 reveal some interesting contrasts.[16] In the parishes of Errigal Truagh, Tydavnet, Clonfeacle, and Desertcreight there was a clear reduction in births which persisted into the 1850s: this was most marked in Tydavnet and Errigal Truagh, where the annual totals halved between 1839–45 and 1847–51. In comparative famine historical terms these reductions are massive, and point to extreme famine conditions in those parishes. The failure of births to recover after the Famine had abated was a product of the scale of mortality and out-migration, and perhaps the persistence of amenorrhoea. In Clonfeacle over the same period the reduction was 24 per cent, and in Desertcreight 27 per cent, but in Seagoe, despite the notable trough in 1847, there was hardly any reduction between the two periods. By the same token the impact of the Famine on Ramoan, Portaferry and Taughboyne was much lighter than in Derryloran.

Only Tydavnet and Desertcreight matched our three Kerry parishes in terms of the fall-off in births. In Kenmare, births plummeted from 334 in 1839–45 to 181 in 1847–53 (and Kenmare's total in the latter period was inflated by baptisms of children born in the workhouse), whereas in Tuosist and Eyeries the number of baptisms was half or less its pre-Famine average in 1847–53. In these Kerry parishes, both the extent of the decline in 1847 and the failure of births to bounce back thereafter are remarkable, and atypical of famines in general.

A New Source on Emigration

Maps 1a and 1b describe the parishes of origin of emigrants who opened an account in the Emigrant Savings Bank in New York City between 1850 and 1858. The bank was founded by Irish-born philanthropists to help their poorer compatriots to place their savings in safe keeping; the savings history of all of those who opened an account between October 1850 and 1858 survive, and they provide information about the origins of savers, the time of their arrival (if immigrants), occupation, address in New York and much more.[17] Map 1a refers to the 1,628 who left Ireland before 1846 while Map 1b refers to the 10,000 or so who might be described as 'Famine emigrants'. In terms of detail on the origin of pre-Famine and Famine-era emigrants, nothing like these maps has existed for Ireland hitherto.

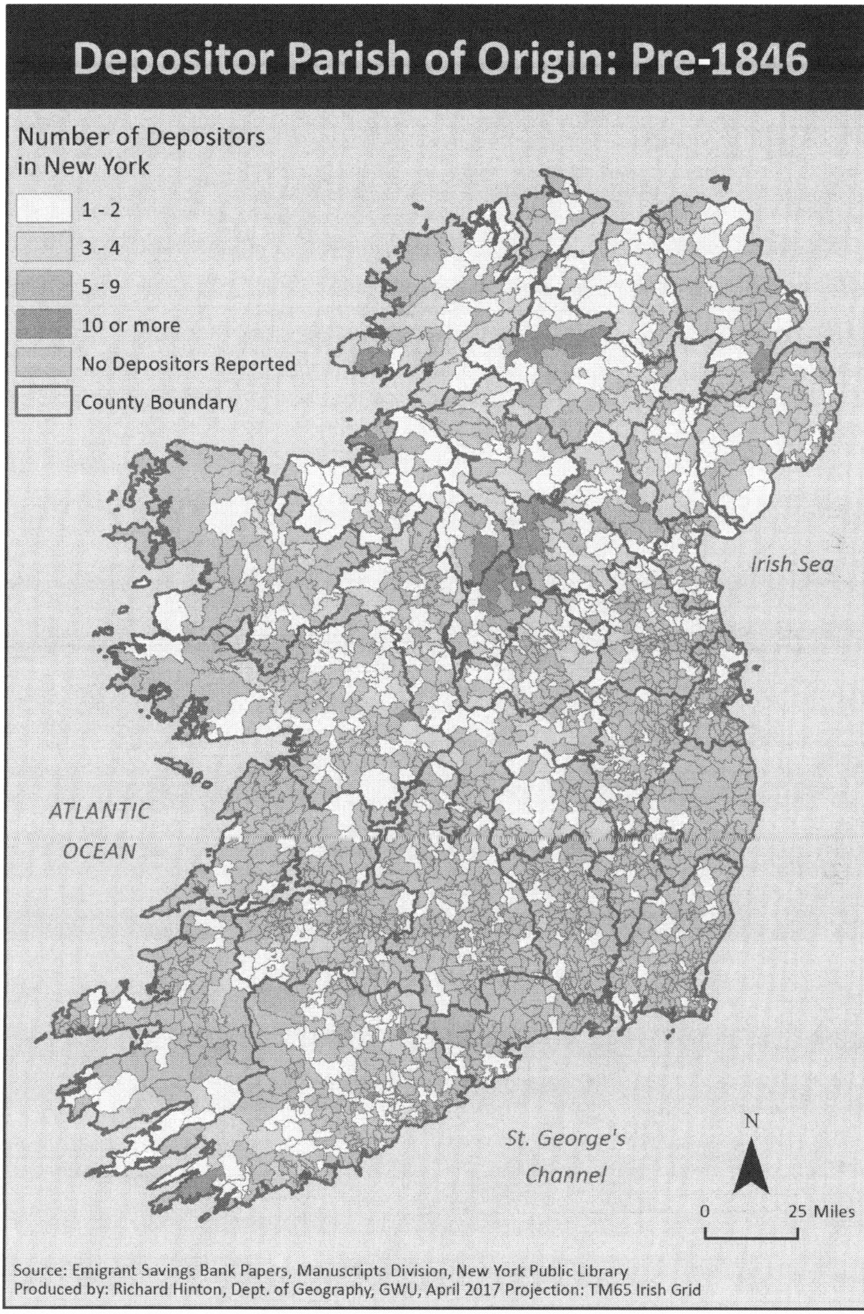
Depositor Parish of Origin: Pre-1846
Number of Depositors in New York
1 - 2
3 - 4
5 - 9
10 or more
No Depositors Reported
County Boundary
Irish Sea
ATLANTIC OCEAN
St. George's Channel
N
0
25 Miles
Source: Emigrant Savings Bank Papers, Manuscripts Division, New York Public Library
Produced by: Richard Hinton, Dept. of Geography, GWU, April 2017 Projection: TM65 Irish Grid

Map 1a

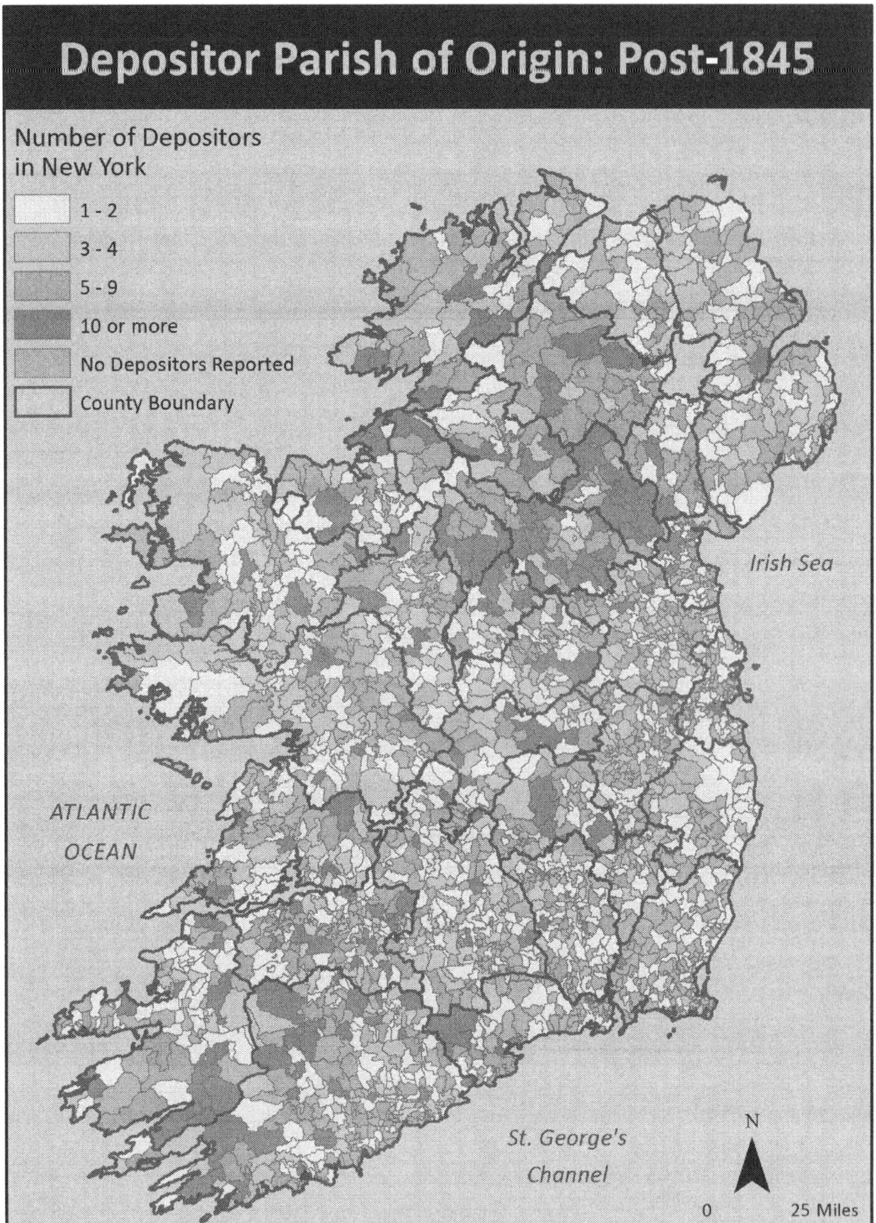
Depositor Parish of Origin: Post-1845
Number of Depositors in New York
1 - 2
3 - 4
5 - 9
10 or more
No Depositors Reported
County Boundary
Irish Sea
ATLANTIC OCEAN
St. George's Channel
N
0
25 Miles
Source: Emigrant Savings Bank Papers, Manuscripts Division, New York Public Library
Produced by: Richard Hinton, Dept. of Geography, GWU, April 2017 Projection: TM65 Irish Grid

Map 1b

Several features stand out. First is the striking persistence of emigration from those parishes which sent out most emigrants before 1846. Second, if we are prepared to accept the map as a very rough guide of broader patterns, a key feature is the almost complete absence in the pre-Famine period of immigrants from east Ulster, Mayo, Galway, all of Munster and all of Leinster south of Drogheda. Reassuringly, there is a considerable overlap between the map and the county pattern suggested by Cousens,[18] which identified a heavy concentration of pre-Famine emigration in west and south Ulster, north-east Connacht, and north Leinster. Cousens inferred out-migration rates from comparing those aged less than 10 years and 11–20 years in 1821 with those aged 21–30 years and 31–40 years in 1841 by county. However, this can be done only at county level.

Comparing Maps 1a and 1b, the continuity of patterns established in the pre-Famine era into the post-1845 period is striking. This calls for some more formal spatial analysis. But note also the implication of more emigration than before from much of the west and south. An obvious caveat is that migrants from places with no EISB (Emigrant Industrial Savings Bank) presence headed elsewhere than New York, to Canada or to Philadelphia. For example, the lack of emigrants from parishes in west Donegal is explained by the preference of those who left places like Ardara and Killybegs for the coalmining districts of Pennsylvania;[19] and the absence of depositors from Gweedore might be explained by the generally low rate of permanent migration from that area, where Scotland to which there was a high rate of seasonal migration – would emerge as the permanent destination of choice.

An intriguing feature of both maps, on which information was previously totally lacking, is the within-county variations. The literature on migration highlights the central role of migration networks and immigrant clusters (e.g. the high concentration of Irish immigrants in parts of New York's Sixth Ward). Our maps pinpoint the persistent clustering also at points of departure; note in particular the clusters of savers in parishes on the borders of Cavan, Leitrim and Longford; in south Monaghan; and in mid-Tyrone. What the maps are silent on is whether there were clusters elsewhere producing no EISB account holders in New York but lots of migrants to places such as Philadelphia, New England and Canada.

Did pre-Famine migration mitigate the impact of the Famine? And if so how: by removing poor people, by providing a reachable destination or by establishing a source of remittances? In what follows I provide one rough-and-ready, non-technical answer based on these EISB data. I define the number of EISB account holders who left before 1846 as a percentage of the 1831 population as a proxy for the emigration rate. My other variable is the rate of population growth between 1821 and 1841 in parishes in seven adjacent counties in Ulster or adjacent to it (Longford, Sligo, Leitrim, Westmeath, Cavan, Monaghan, Fermanagh) where account holders were numerous. The included counties are all inland (setting aside Leitrim's short coastal strip and Sligo's scenic beaches). Across parishes in these seven counties, the variation in the emigration rate, defined as above, helps to predict the rate of population growth. The elasticity (using the mean values of population change between 1821 and 1841 and the emigration rate) is about 0.15; a doubling of the emigration rate (or in the number of account holders) would be associated with a reduction of 15 per cent in the rate of population growth (e.g. from 20 to 17 per cent).[20]

Again, in the same counties, the more account holders' parishes supplied before 1846, the smaller was the population decline in them between 1841 and 1851.[21] Of course, no causal inference is justified here: having more account holders could have made parishes less vulnerable to the Famine, but the presence of account holders could also have been a function of other unidentified factors which would also have reduced vulnerability. Perhaps the fact that people had been able to leave indicated that they were less vulnerable in the first place?

The relatively small numbers involved must not be forgotten. It must be noted too that this kind of exercise is clearly subject to omitted variable bias: after all, population change will also have depended on excluded factors such as the share of employment outside agriculture, literacy, the wage rate or being able to speak English, and clearly more sophisticated analysis is required. Still, these outcomes hint at the possibility that insofar as emigration was a form of disaster relief during the Famine, high emigration before 1846 may have tempered the impact of the crisis in some areas.

Conclusion

Ulster was 'different' in the sense that proportionally fewer people died there during the Famine than in the rest of the island. Its more diversified diet and economy certainly played some part in this. So too, perhaps, did its landed proprietors, who were less likely to be encumbered before the Famine and therefore better positioned to pay rates due and to fund relief, and also less likely to evict when the crisis struck. The percentage of townlands in which land was auctioned in the Incumbered Estates Court in the wake of the Famine – a good measure of financial pressure on landlords before the Famine[22] – was much lower in Ulster than elsewhere; in Ulster's poorest county, Donegal, that percentage was miniscule. In addition, the distribution of landholdings and farm sizes was much less unequal in Ulster, as indicated by the lower ratio of farm labourers to farmers in 1841. In Ulster, the ratio was 1.5 to 1, whereas in the rest of Ireland it was 3 to 1. Equally striking is the variation in population change across the province. As noted earlier, Donegal, and particularly its western parishes, stand out; of Ulster's nine counties, only Derry and Down escaped with proportionally fewer deaths.

Much of the literature on the Famine in Ulster has focused heavily on the role of the poor law and the workhouse regime.[23] While there were exceptions – e.g. McCabe and Ó Gráda have documented gross mismanagement and dereliction in Enniskillen – the system seemed to work better in Ulster than in the rest of Ireland. On the whole, the workhouses were up and running before the potato failed, there was less overcrowding and fewer deaths from infectious diseases, and fewer boards of guardians were dissolved. But the pressures facing the system were also much less than in Mayo or Clare. Indeed, the rate-in-aid act, so controversial in Ulster before its passage in May 1849,[24] was a measure of that. So the issue is to compare like with like, by choosing the appropriate yardstick.[25] It is to be hoped that ongoing and future research at the Ulster University and elsewhere will come to grips with this issue.

Notes

1 Thanks to Breandán Mac Suibhne for very useful comments on an earlier draft. The research that generated the maps in the text was funded by a Collaborative Research Grant (with Tyler Anbinder and Simone Wegge) from the National Endowment for the Humanities.

2 See J. Grant, 'The Great Famine in County Down', in L. Proudfoot (ed.), *Down: History & Society* (Dublin: Geography Publications, 1997), p. 368; J. Grant, 'The Great Famine in the Province of Ulster: The Mechanism of Relief', unpublished PhD dissertation, Queens University Belfast (1986).

3 J. Crowley, W.J. Smyth and M. Murphy (eds), *Atlas of the Great Irish Famine* (Cork: Cork University Press, 2012), p. 19.

4 A.S. Fotheringham, M.H. Kelly and M. Charlton, 'The Demographic Impacts of the Irish Famine: Towards A Greater Geographical Understanding', *Transactions of the Institute of British Geographers*, 38, 2 (2013), Map 2.

5 Mac Suibhne points out that the DED is probably a more meaningful measure than the parish, given the considerable size of parishes in the west and on marginal land. See B.

Mac Suibhne, 'A Jig in the Poor House', *Dublin Review of Books*, 23 April 2013: www.drb.ie/essays/a-jig-in-the-poorhouse (accessed 10 May 2017).

6 See M. Cohen, *Linen, Family, and Community in Tullylish, County Down, 1690–1914* (Dublin: Four Courts Press, 1997); M. Cohen, 'Towards an Historical Ethnography of the Great Irish Famine', in David Nugent (ed.), *Locating Capitalism in Time and Space: Global Restructurings, Politics and Identity* (Stanford, Calif.: Stanford University Press, 2002), pp. 113–36.

7 F.X. McCorry, 'The Montiaghs of North Armagh', *Seanchas Ardmhacha, Journal of the Armagh Diocesan Historical Society*, 18, 2 (2001), pp. 148–52.

8 Ibid. pp. 150–2.

9 B. Mac Suibhne, '"Bastard Ribbonism": The Molly Maguires, the Uneven Failure of Entitlements and the Politics of Post-Famine Adjustment', in E. Delaney and B. Mac Suibhne (eds), *Ireland's Great Famine and Popular Politics* (London: Routledge, 2016), pp. 186–231.

10 J. Mokyr, *Why Ireland Starved*, 2nd edition (London: Allen & Unwin, 1985). See also J. Mokyr, 'The Deadly Fungus: An Econometric Investigation into the Short-Term Demographic Impact of the Irish Famine, 1846–1851', *Research in Population Economics*, vol. 2 (1980), pp. 237–77.

11 C. Ó Gráda, '"The Last, the Most Dreadful Resource of Nature": Economic–Historical Reflections on Famine', *Atlantic Economic Journal*, 44, 2 (2016), pp. 225–41.

12 G. Alfani, *Calamities and the Economy in Renaissance Italy: The Grand Tour of the Horsemen of the Apocalypse* (Basingstoke: Palgrave Macmillan, 2013).

13 Available from Catholic Parish Registers at the National Library of Ireland: http://registers.nli.ie.

14 Even when complete, some of the registers are extremely hard to read, though this matters less when only a monthly count is needed. Some contain gaps in the 1840s, e.g. data are lacking for Glenravel between late September 1841 and early October 1848.

15 Available from Parish Registers at the Representative Church Body Library: https://www.ireland.anglican.org/about/rcb-library/online-parish-records.

16 The data are further described in Figure 1 of C. Ó Gráda, 'Notes on the Demography of the Famine in Ulster', UCD Centre for Economic Research Working Paper 2017-13.

17 See T. Anbinder, S. Wegge and C. Ó Gráda, 'The Savings, Mobility, and Networks of New York's Irish Famine Immigrants: Preliminary Evidence from the Emigrant Savings Bank' (forthcoming, 2017); C. Ó Gráda, 'The Famine, the New York Irish, and their Bank', in A.E. Murphy and R. Prendergast (eds), *Contributions to the History of Economic Thought: Essays in Honour of R.D.C. Black* (London: Routledge, 2000), pp. 227–48.

18 S.H. Cousens, 'The Regional Variations in Emigration from Ireland between 1821 and 1841', *Transactions of the Institute of British Geographers*, 37 (1965), pp. 15–30.

19 B. Mac Suibhne, 'Them Poor Irish Lads in Pennsylvania', *Dublin Review of Books*, 1 March 2015: www.drb.ie/essays/'them-poor-irish-lads'-in-pennsylvania [note: the inverted commas in this address must not be changed to 'smart quotes' or the URL won't work] (accessed 10 May 2017).

20 I have also checked the impact of excluding parishes with no EISB account holders; this makes no difference.

21 In this case I have added a dummy variable valued at 1 if there was a workhouse in the parish.

22 A. Eiríksson and C. Ó Gráda, *Estate Records of the Irish Famine* (Dublin: Irish Famine Network, 1995); A. Eiríksson and C. Ó Gráda, 'Bankrupt Landlords and the Irish Famine', in C. Ó Gráda, *Ireland's Great Famine: Interdisciplinary Perspectives* (Dublin: UCD Press, 2006), pp. 48–62.

23 See J. Vincent, 'A Political Orchestration of the Irish Famine: County Fermanagh 1847', in M. Silverman and P.H. Gulliver (eds), *Approaching the Past: Historical Anthropology Through Irish Case Studies* (New York: Columbia University Press, 1992), pp. 75–98; C. Kinealy and T. Parkhill, *The Famine in Ulster* (Belfast: Ulster Historical Foundation, 1997); B. Logan, *Ballymena During the Great Famine* (Ballymena: Brian Logan, 2000); G. Mac Atasney, *'This Dreadful Visitation': The Famine in Lurgan/Portadown* (Dublin: Beyond the Pale, 1997); B. McDonald, 'A Time of Desolation: Clones Poor Law Union 1845-50', *Clogher Record*, 17, 1 (2000), pp. 3–146; D. McCabe and C. Ó Gráda, 'Destitution, Human Agency, and Relief: Enniskillen Workhouse During the Irish Famine', in M. Denie and S. Farrell (eds), *Power and Popular Culture in Modern Ireland: Essays in Honour of James S. Donnelly, Jr.* (Dublin: Irish Academic Press, 2010), pp. 7–30.

24 J. Grant, 'The Great Famine and the Poor Law in Ulster: The Rate-in-Aid Issue of 1849', *Irish Historical Studies*, 27, 105 (1990), pp. 30–47.

25 See T. Guinnane and C. Ó Gráda, 'Workhouse Mortality and the Great Irish Famine', in T. Dyson and C. Ó Gráda, *Famine Demography: Perspectives from the Past and Present* (Oxford: Oxford University Press, 2002), pp. 44–64; C. Ó Gráda, 'Yardsticks for Workhouse Management During the Great Famine', in V. Crossman and P. Gray (eds), *Poverty and Welfare in Ireland 1838–1948* (Dublin: Irish Academic Press, 2011), pp. 69–96.

Chapter Three

The Famine Irish Migration to Canada in 1847–8: Assisted Emigration, Colonisation and the Unpublished Famine Diaries of Stephen De Vere[1]

Jason King

On St Patrick's Day, 1847, the Anglo-Irish landowner Stephen De Vere was hailed by 5,000 people at his estate at Curragh Chase in Country Limerick as 'the best friend that the poor man ever had; the protector of the widow and the orphan'.[2] As he stood before the assembled crowd, De Vere stated: 'I have … made up my mind to emigrate to Upper Canada about the middle of April, taking with me some of my people … who have been pauperized by the loss of the potato crop'.[3] Four days earlier, he had written to his uncle, Lord Monteagle, claiming that 'I propose to take out, in the first instance, only my own household labourers, & to possess myself of a tract of land partly cleared, & partly wild, in Upper Canada, in the immediate neighbourhood of the uncultivated districts'.[4] As Peter Gray has noted, 'liberal Protestant Irish landlords such as [Stephen's younger brother, the poet Aubrey] De Vere and Lord Monteagle sincerely believed that the interests of the colonies and Ireland were complementary and mutually realizable through systematic colonization'.[5] In *Sending Out Ireland's Poor: Assisted Emigration to North America in the Nineteenth Century*, Gerard Moran examines the development of these assisted emigration and colonisation schemes in parliamentary papers and reports, and under the auspices of the Irish landlords, the British government and the poor law. However, unlike other proponents of assisted emigration, De Vere personally escorted former tenants to British North America in order to put his ideas into practice:

> [T]he supporters of emigration were strong in their conviction – Stephen De Vere of Curragh Chase, Co. Limerick, was so adamant that such a project would be a success that in [April] 1847 he set off for Canada on a fact-finding mission. Prior to his departure he told an audience in Pallaskenry, Co. Limerick, that his aim was to see a movement on an extensive scale that would benefit both countries.[6]

This chapter examines Stephen De Vere's unpublished diary entries and letters concerning his attempt to establish a model for colonial resettlement in Canada West in 1847–8 as a means of famine relief and alleviating class conflict.[7] The first part tracks De Vere's Famine voyage to Quebec and Ontario in 1847–8 and his descriptions of the Canadian landscapes and early patterns of settlement. His unpublished Famine diaries and journals remain almost completely unknown yet represent some of the most compelling and vivid Canadian travel narratives of the mid-Victorian period.[8] The second part of the chapter considers how De Vere earned his moniker as the 'protector of the widow and the orphan' by attesting to their suffering with harrowing eyewitness testimony that shocked British Parliamentarians into reforming the Passenger Acts. More specifically, it argues that De Vere differed from other advocates of colonisation insofar as he personally experienced the hardships of the transatlantic voyage alongside former tenants from his estate on their journey to London, Ontario. Indeed, he tried to put into practice ideas expressed by his younger brother Aubrey in his pamphlet 'Colonization' (1850). Here, Aubrey De Vere avowed that through 'colonization nations are enabled to retrieve the past, [to remedy] an estate burdened by the original sin of accumulated pauperism'.[9] The chapter suggests that De Vere's attempt to expiate Ireland's 'original sin' through emigration failed because he sought to recreate its hierarchical, semi-feudal class relations on Canadian soil, whereas his former tenants often preferred waged labour and moved to the United States, or were emboldened by the Young Ireland uprising of 1848. More broadly, it contends that De Vere's personal failure to resettle Famine emigrants had policy implications in compounding the lack of political will to fund colonisation schemes, even when it seemed a distinct possibility[10] and his recommendations for Passenger Act reform were accepted in 1848. Ultimately, De Vere was dismayed that the very legislation he inspired to safeguard emigrants at sea increased Canadian immigration taxes and thereby stymied the passenger trade he had sought to promote.

Stephen De Vere is at once the most influential and least understood eyewitness of the Irish Famine migration of 1847. On 30 November 1847, he wrote a letter in Toronto to Thomas Frederick Elliot that was reproduced in the British Parliamentary Papers and remains the most widely cited description of the Famine voyage. In De Vere's own words:

> Before the emigrant has been a week at sea he is an altered man. How could it be otherwise? Hundreds of poor people, men, women, and children of all ages from the drivelling idiot of ninety to the babe just born, huddled together without light, without air, wallowing in filth and breathing a fetid atmosphere, sick in body, dispirited in heart, the fevered patients lying between the sound in sleeping places so narrow as almost to deny them the power of indulging, by a change of position, the natural restlessness of the disease, by their agonized ravings disturbing those around them and predisposing them, through the effects of the imagination, to imbibe the contagion; living without food or medicine except as administered by the hand of casual charity, dying without the voice of spiritual consolation and buried in the deep without the rites of the Church.[11]

According to Aubrey De Vere, Stephen had risked his life when:

> [H]e took passage for Canada with a considerable number of those who had been employed … under his supervision, and conducted them to Quebec, sharing with them all the sufferings and perils which then belonged to a crowded steerage passage. Those who escaped fever on their sea-passage frequently caught it on landing, the dormant seeds of disease becoming rapidly developed by the stimulus of better air and food, and by infection. It was so on this occasion. They reached Quebec in June of 1847, and in a short time nearly all of those whom he had taken with him and lodged in a large, healthy house were stricken down in succession, during a period covering about eight months, and received from him personally all the ministrations which they could have had from a hospital nurse ... His letter describing the sufferings of emigrants was read aloud in the House of Lords by Earl Grey, then Secretary for the Colonies, and the 'Passengers Act' was amended, due

> accommodations of all sorts being provided in the emigrant vessels. Most of those emigrants who on reaching Quebec went into the crowded and infected hospitals died there. It is impossible to guess how many thousands of emigrants may have been saved by this enterprise.[12]

Indeed, De Vere's eyewitness testimony was instrumental in bringing about Passenger Act reform. In his classic study of the Passenger Acts, Oliver MacDonagh contends that 'it is scarcely too much to regard it as the basis of most of their future legislation for ship life.'[13] Despite his influence, however, the fact that Stephen De Vere kept copious journals and wrote extensive letters during his voyage to Canada in 1847–8 remains little known. The small red journal in which he jotted down his impressions on a daily basis is one of the most important documents relating to Irish Famine migration and an invaluable cultural and historical resource. His first entry for the voyage is dated 1 May 1847, and the only thing that he writes is 'sailed'; the next one is 9 June, when De Vere remarks that his passenger vessel, the *Birman*, is 'Off Cape Breton in sight of land[,] having reached the banks of Newfoundland June 3rd.'[14] It is not until the *Birman* reaches Grosse Isle on 16 June 1847, that he begins to write lengthier entries into his journal:

> Arrived at Grosse isle quarantine about 7 am. Detained waiting for dr till evening, when he inspected & gave us clean bill of health – abt. 40 ships detained there villages of white tents on shore for the sick. Daily mortality about 150. One ship, Sisters of Liverpool, in with all passengers & crew in fever of this ship, all but the Cap'n and one girl died.
>
> Laid alongside of 'Jessy' in which many ill. Water covered with beds, cooking utensils refuse of the dead. Ghastly appearance of boats full of sick going ashore never to return. Several died between ship and shore. Wives separated from husbands, children from parents. Ascertained by subsequent enquiry that funds in agents hands altogether insufficient for care. Medical attendance bad. Exemplary conduct of Catholic Clergy.[15]

Stephen De Vere's diary entries are evocative and emotionally gripping, but provide the detailed observations of a genuine Famine migrant. He outlines many of the themes – the cursory medical inspections at Grosse Isle, the inadequacy of medical attention or living quarters for the sick, the exemplary conduct of the Roman Catholic clergy – that he would later expound upon in his letter to T.F. Elliot. As the *Birman* lay at anchor off Grosse Isle, De Vere bears witness to the grim traffic all around him of small vessels ferrying the sick and the dead from the 'coffin ships' to the fever sheds and mass graves on the island. His journal records the spectacle of sundered families, that moment of separation in which Irish children are orphaned and left bereft of their parents.

After he left Grosse Isle, De Vere remained a keen observer of his surroundings as he travelled upriver. He arrived in Quebec City the next day, on 17 June, where he lodged a complaint against the ship's captain, donated the £10 fine 'for the use of destitute Emigrants' and noted that the 'Irish and [French-]Canadians dislike one another'.[16] At 6 a.m. on 24 June, De Vere reached Montreal, where he observed: 'Frightful mortality in the Emigrant Sheds hospitals & generally Throughout the town'.[17] He remained in Montreal until 13 July and then embarked for Toronto, marvelling at the beauty of the Canadian countryside from the deck of his steamship, especially around a Thousand Islands. In his own words:

> From Brockville to Kingston. This an archipelago of islands. Perfect labyrinth. The larger ones with large trees. The smaller ones with brushwood & dwarf pines. Landed in one. Beautiful andromeda. Narrow channels where hardly room for steamers suddenly spreading out. Great inland seas, & then as suddenly contracted. Lavish profusion of vegetation. The most barren rock has its tree – tree arboretum. At Kingston change steamers. New fortifications Kingston in a great scale for the protection of harbour. Immense crowd of German and Irish Emigrants on board of the worst description. Great apparent disease. Pay difference for cabin Passage to Toronto $6. Pass Cobourg and Port Hope at night. Wednesday July 14th Arrive at Toronto at 11am.[18]

His first impression of Toronto was of St Michael's nearly completed 'Magnificent Catholic Cathedral … building. Brick with cut stone door'.[19]

De Vere remained in Ontario for the year following July 1847, though his plan to purchase land and establish a settlement near London never came to fruition. He was a keen observer of Canadian colonial growth and the cultivation of the wilderness. Indeed, De Vere was especially interested in the varieties of Canadian foliage, as his estate at Curragh Chase is in an area of old growth, hardwood forest – now a state-owned Coillte forest park – with its own arboretum. On 17 July 1847, De Vere travelled by stage to Holland Landing:

> The country from Toronto northwards to Holland landing where the stage stops exhibits the back country in every stage of improvement. You have the wild forest – trees of enormous height & girth, but furnished with few & short branches – groves of the graceful hemlock and balsam spruce[,] a rich thicket underwood of hemlock and aborite, here called the cedar – occasional elms as tall and straight as the pines – Ash, walnut, beech, sugar maple, thickets of sumach with leaves of great size, crowned with spikes of crimson flowers. Then the past stages of improvement where the underwood has been cut down and lucent [?] round the stems of the giant pines, now dead & blackened – all around the scene of smoking desolation. Great trees lying over the ground – then, the rich crops of corn growing amongst the bare Trunks. In the neat stage, the trees have been cut down to within about 3 feet of the surface with luxuriant drops of meadow between the logs piled into burned fences & for log huts or shanties – lastly the rich & highly cultivated farms (always however backed by the eternal forest) with its neat farm house framed, whitewashed, & its flourishing orchard – government are making a great road from Toronto to Holland landing.[20]

Through De Vere's eyes, the cultivation of the Canadian forests was seen in each stage of its development. He witnessed the early spread of Toronto into its luxuriant woodlands and encroachment on the receding wilderness. More broadly, De Vere was highly sensitive to the Canadian landscapes he observed as he travelled extensively through Canada West in 1847–48. His impressions of Niagara Falls on 25 May 1848 are beautifully rendered over several pages in his journals and letters,[21] as are his records of everyday Canadian life at that time, whether it is Christmas festivities,[22] his frequent hunting excursions, his encounters with First Nations peoples on 23 June 1848,[23] or of trying to purchase a farm in the early settlement of London.[24] What recurs again and again in the unpublished De Vere journals are his perceptions and feelings of joy at the beauty of the Canadian landscape.

Ultimately, however, De Vere did not purchase land or remain in Canada West. In fact, he had an ulterior motive for his migration. As he wrote to his elder brother, Vere Edmond, on 11 February 1848:

> In my letters home I have left one thing unsaid, which is for you alone. You know what had been for a considerable time (8 or 9 years) the tendency of my religious opinions. I could no longer, when thrown independently upon the world, reconcile it to my conscience to conceal them & I have, since I reached America, conformed to the ordinances of the Catholic Church. Whether this has got wind at home, or not I do not know. My principal reason for leaving my own country was to save my mother the pain which I feared the avowal of my convictions would have caused to her, nor will I ever reside in Ireland if that avowal gives her more pain than my presence would give pleasure ... I leave the matter wholly in your hands to disclose or conceal as you think best for my mother. Should your reply be unfavourable, I am determined, at any cost, to remain an exile for conscience sake. If favourable, being 'functus officis' here, & having probably laid the foundation of much benefit to my native land, I am ready to return and share the fortunes of my family & home; but I will never live again at home concealing my faith, a faith from which I have derived strength to bear every hardship & consolation under every misfortune & privation.[25]

There is no record of a reply to De Vere's letter, but it must have been favourable because he did return to Ireland in 1848 as an openly practising Catholic, facilitating Aubrey De Vere's conversion a few years later.

As a convert to Catholicism, a proponent of assisted emigration and a philanthropic colonist who personally led his former tenants to resettle in British North America, Stephen De Vere hardly fits the stereotype of the absentee proprietor or rapacious landlord. Yet he was highly atypical in regard to his relationship with his former tenants, as he himself came to realise. De Vere's papers indicate that he decided not to purchase land because of their increasing sense of disaffection, 'disrespectful'[26] attitude, and defections to the US. In his own words, written in a letter on 12 April 1848, 'every man of them becomes an American sympathizer', 'a bitter enemy to England, + to the Anglo-Canadian connection[,] ... + every man, through the relation which he carefully keeps up with his old country, contributes to increase Irish disaffection.'[27] De Vere perceived republican sentiment to be widespread among the Famine Irish and feared it could be mobilised by a host of potential enemies.

He also developed feelings of deep contempt for Americans on his journeys to the US. In Rochester, New York, on 3 September 1847, De Vere wrote that:

> My impressions hitherto of the Americans is that they are the Hungriest, the dirtiest, the most dishonest & altogether the meanest people I have ever seen. They are so entirely absorbed in the pursuit of wealth that they have no time for the courtesies, the decencies of life. They cry 'O my ducats'! without 'O my daughter'! They seem to rely wholly on themselves, never brushing with their neighbours. Their dishonesty is audacious, because they are too vain to attempt to conceal it; & whilst they are cheating you, they do not even pay you the poor compliment of trying to deceive you. Proud of their country, (because she belongs to themselves) they are most proud of her meanest vices. An expert windbag is honoured and as a smart man.[28]

De Vere's contempt for American individualism in the US reinforced his sense of loyalty to British North America, but increasingly not as a destination for himself.

He was also particularly disturbed while abroad by the upheaval of the Young Ireland movement, culminating in the uprising which was led by his brother-in-law, William Smith O'Brien, in 1848. When he learned on 10 April of O'Brien's role in fomenting unrest, De Vere described his 'motives' as 'always pure, honorable + patriotic', though he was 'dazzled by the wonderful progress of Revolutionary principle over all Europe' that 'allowed him to be hurried to the pitch of revolutionary folly'.[29] The agitation also caused a conflict of loyalties for De Vere himself, who wrote to Aubrey on 14 May 1848:

> People may say I remain absent and this is cowardice, [but] you fully appreciate the extreme pain of the position in which I should be placed if home at present. I could not + would not be disloyal even if I thought the rising had a chance of success; but I never could bring myself to aid in spilling the blood of the noble deluded people who are entwined with my heart strings.[30]

De Vere felt a sense of divided allegiance between loyalty to crown and country, and his love of the 'noble, deluded people' who did not reciprocate his affection. In his view, their delusions were inspired by republican ideals that exacerbated social divisions and aggravated political tensions which he had hoped but failed to resolve through emigration to Canada.

Nevertheless, De Vere increasingly came to admire the Canadian caregivers of the Famine Irish,[31] especially people like emigration agent

Edward McElderry and Toronto's Bishop Michael Power, to both of whom he paid tribute. He also bore witness to the intense suffering of the Famine Irish in Ontario. On 20 November 1847, he wrote:

> A family from Mayo came out this year apparently in the most abject poverty. They consisted of a father mother uncle a little boy about 12 years old. They were transmitted to Toronto at the govt. expense. The mother was there taken into hospital suffering from a rapid cancer in the breast. She soon died. The father, uncle, little boy took a poor lodging close to me. I frequently met them and the father complaining to me of dysentery. I recommended him to send for a doctor, but he said he was too poor. He at last went into hospital, and died, from want of care in the early stage of the disease, leaving his little son in possession of 300 sovereigns tied up in an old rag, which had, during the voyage, been tied under the mother's breast and had produced the cancer of which she died.[32]

Moreover, on 9 January 1848, De Vere was in Port Stanley when he observed:

> [A] beggar in a lonely part of the bush heading towards an old burial ground [with] three coffins, [one for each of his daughters] who had all died together of fever. So great was the fear of infection that none of the neighbours would attend the funeral. The old father … with the assistance of his wife, herself in fever, dug his daughters' graves & buried their remains. In a few days the wife died, & the old man still survives, the last of his race.[33]

These diary entries were never intended for public consumption, but reinforce the impression of Irish emigrants in the Canadas as objects of fear and loathing. Indeed, earlier on 18 September, De Vere had noted in his journal that emigration agent 'McElderry mentions that the farmers in the country are raising subscriptions to send back the emigrants into Toronto.'[34] According to the *British Canadian* newspaper, De Vere 'had rendered much assistance … [to] McElderry, boarding with him every steamer filled with the wretched cargoes, and transmitting to the "proper authorities" the result of his laborious experience.'[35] On 6 November 1847, De Vere wrote: 'I regret to hear of poor McElderry's death of fever at Toronto.'[36]

He was also stricken by the death of Bishop Michael Power, whom De Vere recorded on 29 September was 'very ill of typhus fever'. He was in Toronto on 1 October when Bishop Power passed away. De Vere recorded this in a very moving private obituary:

> Rev. Michael Power Cath bishop of Toronto died this morning. He was a man of great generosity and nobleness, most kindly and charitable in a true and most extended kindly sense, an humble Christian. By his example, his justice, his unfailing attention to the duties of his high station, & the strictness of his discipline, he brought into perfect order a diocese which he found almost in anarchy. His death is attributable, under providence, to the noble and devoted zeal with which, since the illness of so many of his clergy, he has visited the beds of every sick and dying emigrant. He did not spare himself, but God has spared him a longer sojourn on earth. He was a man of no political party, of no religious bigotry. He was too strong-minded to be a bigot, & too wise to be a partisan. He was therefore respected and beloved by men of all creeds and parties. May Almighty God have Mercy on his soul.[37]

De Vere did not forget McElderry and Bishop Power's compassion, devotion and self-sacrifice. Several years later, in Limerick, he recalled their heroism: 'when in Toronto, disease had so thinned the ranks of the priesthood that now [none] but the Bishop remained to do the duty of visiting the sick, that excellent man instantly undertook it. He laboured unremittingly, and died of fever within a fortnight'.[38]

Ultimately, Stephen De Vere was inspired by the Canadian caregivers of the Famine Irish such as Bishop Power and Edward McElderry, who were to be commemorated in Dr. George Robert Grasett Park in Toronto. He also increasingly saw it as his role to bear witness to the suffering of Irish emigrants and to remedy their plight. His famous letter exposing the harrowing conditions on 'coffin ships', read aloud by Lord Grey in the House of Lords, can be traced to De Vere's unpublished diary entries and the letters written in Toronto. De Vere's journal entry on 19 July 1847 reads: 'wrote a paper describing the treatment of passengers on board emigrant ships with sundry suggestions for ensuring better arrangements'.[39] On 30 November, he records 'preparing dispatch' and then 'dispatch my letter' the following day.[40] Two months later, on 12 February 1848, De Vere notes with satisfaction: 'a report of a public meeting in Toronto, adopting almost verbatim my views as to the necessity of improvement in the emigration system. Thus I have the satisfaction of finding my opinions supported by the Canadian public, & at the same time likely to be adopted by the English ministry.'[41]

Indeed, the very moment his impressions of the 'coffin ships' began to shape government policy was recorded in a letter on 31 January 1848 from Eliot Warbourton to Aubrey De Vere. 'I was at the Colonial Office on Saturday, where I found its secretary [Lord Grey] … in raptures', Warbourton writes, 'about a letter he had received from Stephen. He said [it] was just what he wanted in stating his experience in his brave enterprise of emigrating as a pauper – he had "made the dumb to speak"'.[42] In 'emigrating as a pauper' and ostensibly giving 'the dumb' a voice, De Vere defined the lasting image of the 'coffin ship' and helped shape 'future legislation' for emigrant protection.[43] He registered the predicament of migrants in transit that led to a change in policy.

Even so, De Vere was dismayed that the legislation he inspired increased levies for emigrant ships that undermined the passenger trade he had sought to safeguard.[44] His protestations about migrants in peril helped shape policy but simultaneously closed off avenues of escape from Ireland. De Vere remained highly conscious of his role in stimulating emigrant legislation that inadvertently stymied future colonisation schemes. He took particular exception to the idea that dependent women and children, who were stigmatised in the Canadian press,[45] would inevitably remain paupers if assisted to emigrate to British North America. As he wrote to Lord Monteagle on 29 February 1848:

> Even widows, with their children, may be able to support themselves by their labour, and, at the same time, contribute to the wellbeing of the colony. I know the case of a widow who arrived last year in Toronto, entirely without funds, accompanied by her three boys, 11, 13, & 15 years old. She is now a servant in a respectable family, & her three little boys have obtained permanent employment ... An able-bodied labourer, in Ireland, may be a pauper, unable to support his wife, parents, or children; but in Canada, where wages are high, & where I say fearlessly, the labour market will provide profitable employment for an emigration greater than any which has yet reached her shore, neither the able-bodied labourer nor the helpless members of his family can be considered as paupers.[46]

Gerard Moran notes that De Vere's views would be vindicated when 'demand for female domestic servants in Canada' significantly increased in the 1850s,[47] but they were perceived as a burden and a threat in the immediate aftermath of the Famine migration.

While he resided in Ontario in 1847–8, De Vere also closely followed British Parliamentary and Canadian colonial debates about emigrant legislation. In a letter to his mother on 10 April, he claimed that the Colonial Secretary 'Lord Grey's dispatches against emigration was a miserable attempt to cajole Canada through her worst prejudices; but a crooked policy does not always produce the results contemplated by the most gracious desires'. He also informed her of his intention to 'break up my establishment here' and return to Ireland because his colonisation scheme has not been a success.[48] One month later, on 14 May, De Vere complained to Aubrey that:

> Lord Grey's conduct has been extremely weak and mean. To show himself against the pressure of public opinion at home in favor of emigration, he writes a dispatch to [Canadian Governor General] Lord Elgin on the 1st Dec. (a dispatch bad in feeling, hasty, puerile in its details) in which he gives the outline of a measure restrictive of emigration to be instantly hurried through the Canadian Legislature … Base and unstatesmanlike![49]

De Vere was even more scathing about Lord Grey's 'crooked system of unwise & illiberal policy' in a letter he published in the *Western Canadian* newspaper on 16 June 1848.[50] Ultimately, his protests fell on deaf ears and the legislation he had inspired came to pass.

Nevertheless, Stephen De Vere was the most influential advocate of the emigrant's protection and chronicler of their plight. Before his departure from Canada, he was praised in the *Church* newspaper as a 'zealous and devoted man' who 'merits the thanks of the people of this Province', according to the *British Canadian*.[51] 'In Toronto he closely and frequently inspected the Hospital sheds, crowded as they were with contagious fever, and accompanied the Emigrant Agent [McElderry] in his visits to Steamers as they arrived with their loads of passengers, and to the Emigrants Sheds', reported the *Toronto Patriot* on 23 May 1848. It added that 'Mr. De Vere carries with him the esteem and affection of all who know him personally, and the high respect and ardent good wishes of those to whom he is known only by character.'[52] In correspondence with G. Widder on 8 June 1848, De

Vere acknowledged the growing influence of his letter after it was read aloud in the House of Lords and published. He claims:

> I was greatly surprised by finding that, on the publication of my letter, there was so little to be found fault with, here, in the opinions I put forward. My views were entirely adopted here and founded only on my own observations, & on information obtained generally from humble but practical sources. I had read hardly anything of others' plans, & my long attendance, for months, at the bedside of members of my household, during severe successions in fevers, had shown me out from general or political society. Nor did I for a moment contemplate the publication of my letter.[53]

His motive for writing the letter, he suggests, was solely to help protect Irish emigrants in transit like his former tenants. 'The people I brought out were principally labourers, whom I had employed for many years, & whose condition, from long natural attachment, I was anxious to better,' De Vere adds.[54] After he returned to Ireland, De Vere became an M.P. for Limerick from 1854 to 1859 and then High Sherriff of the county; he also suffered from terrible nightmares which led him to 'lamentable howls' on a nightly basis.[55] He relocated from Curragh Chase to the island of Monare, Foynes, County Limerick, where he spent his later years living as a notable eccentric in a labourer's cottage.

Ultimately, Stephen De Vere's legacy was to help safeguard Irish emigrants at sea *and* to stymie the passenger trade he had sought to promote. Although he claimed to have 'read hardly anything of others' plans', he had originally set out to put into practice a colonisation scheme of his own. The intense suffering he witnessed at sea, in the fever sheds on Grosse Isle, in Montreal, and in Toronto no doubt gave him pause. Shortly after he sent the letter that was read aloud by Lord Grey in the House of Lords De Vere conceded to Aubrey on 23 December 1847 that 'I have not found any opportunity of settling in Upper Canada with any prospect of advantage'.[56] He was also dismayed by his former tenants' 'disrespectful' attitude and claimed, on 23 November 1847, that 'it is fortunate for me that I did not purchase a farm in the expectation of their performing their contract'.[57] Moreover, his decision to return to Ireland was almost certainly motivated by his family's acceptance of his conversion to Catholicism, although there is no surviving document informing him of this. In short, if De Vere is the most influential of the Famine migrants, then his motivations and extensive eyewitness testimonies remain poorly understood. His unpublished correspondence and journals provide an invaluable and unknown record of the Irish Famine migration of 1847 and mid-Victorian travelogue. Both his letter to T.F. Elliot and his failure to resettle former tenants had policy implications in giving expression to the harrowing conditions on the 'coffin ships' and licence to Lord Grey to resist pressure from cabinet colleagues, such as Lord Russell, to implement a state-sponsored emigration scheme in the face of negative Canadian sentiment.[58] The legislation De Vere inspired reduced both the risk and scope of Irish migration to Canada.

Notes

1 Research funding for this chapter was provided by Ireland Park Foundation in Toronto, which I am grateful to acknowledge.

2 *Limerick Reporter*, 2 April 1847.

3 Trinity College Dublin [hereafter, TCD], MS 5075, p. 1846.

4 TCD, MS 5053, p. 4.

5 P. Gray, '"Shovelling out your paupers": The British State and Irish Famine Migration, 1846–50', *Patterns of Prejudice*, 33, 4 (1999), pp. 47–65, 51.

6 G. Moran, *Sending Out Ireland's Poor: Assisted Emigration to North America in the Nineteenth Century* (Dublin: Four Courts, 2004), p. 72.

7 Also see M. McGowan, *Death or Canada: The Irish Famine Migration to Toronto, 1847* (Toronto: Novalis, 2009).

8 One reason De Vere's unpublished Famine diaries are so little known is that the genre has remained under a veneer of suspicion since the publication of Gerald Keegan's fraudulent best-seller, *Famine Diary: Journey to a New World* (Dublin: Wolfhound Press, 1991), a fabricated text that Mark McGowan and I have examined in considerable detail. Unlike *Famine Diary*, De Vere's Famine journals are genuine. See J. King, 'The Genealogy of *Famine Diary* in Ireland and Quebec: Ireland's Famine Migration in Historical Fiction, Historiography, and Memory', *Éire-Ireland*, 47 (2012), pp. 45–69; M. McGowan, 'Famine, Facts, and Fabrication: An Examination of Diaries from the Irish Famine Migration to Canada', *Canadian Journal of Irish Studies*, 33, 2 (2007), pp. 48–55.

9 'Aubrey De Vere, Colonization', *Edinburgh Review*, 91 (1850), pp. 54–5.

10 Gray, 'Shovelling out your paupers', pp. 63–5; G. Moran, *Sending Out Ireland's Poor*, pp. 83–90.

11 T.F. Elliot testified before the Select Committee of the House of Lords on Colonization from Ireland and entered Stephen De Vere's letter of 30 November 1847 into the Minutes of Evidence on 9 March 1848. *First Report from the House of Lords Select Committee on Colonization from Ireland; Together with the Minutes of Evidence*, p. 45. Also reproduced in *Minutes of Evidence before Select Committee on Colonization from Ireland, letter to the Select Committee* (30 November 1847) in *British Parliamentary Papers, Emigration*, vol. 5 (Shannon: Irish University Press, 1968), pp. 45–8.

12 A. De Vere, *Recollections of Aubrey De Vere* (London: Edward Arnold, 1897), p. 253.
13 O. MacDonagh, *A Pattern of Government Growth: Passenger Acts and their Enforcement, 1800–1860* (London: MacGibbon & Gee, 1961), p. 191.
14 TCD, MS 5061, vol. 1 (29 August–1 December 1847), p. 1.
15 Ibid. pp. 2–3.
16 Ibid. p. 4.
17 Ibid. p. 7.
18 Ibid. pp. 14–15.
19 Ibid. p. 16.
20 Ibid. pp. 17–18.
21 TCD, MS 5062, vol. 2 (1 December 1847–23 June 1848), pp. 48–50.
22 Ibid. p. 4.
23 Ibid. p. 55–7.
24 TCD, MS 5061, vol. 1 (29 August–1 December 1847), p. 55; MS 5062, vol. 2 (1 December 1847–23 June 1848), pp. 5, 12, 14, 24.
25 TCD, MS 5075a, pp. 81–2.
26 TCD, MS 5061, vol. 1, p. 55.
27 TCD, MS 5075a/2 (1847), p. 133.
28 TCD, MS 5061, vol. 1, pp. 31–2.
29 TCD, MS 5075a, pp. 135, 163.
30 Ibid. p. 152.
31 Also see J. King, 'Remembering and Forgetting the Famine Irish in Quebec: Genuine and False Memoirs, Communal Memory, and Migration', *Irish Review*, 44 (2012), pp. 20–41, 31–4, for Stephen De Vere's admiration of female religious orders such as the Grey Nuns in Montreal.
32 TCD, MS 5061, vol. 1, p. 54.
33 TCD, MS 5062, vol. 2, p. 8. Also see MS 5061, vol. 1, p. 54.
34 TCD, MS 5062, vol. 2, p. 37.
35 TCD, MS 5073; *British Canadian* (May 20, 1848), p. 1.
36 TCD, MS 5061, vol. 1, p. 49.
37 Ibid. pp. 40–1.
38 TCD, MS 5074/3, pp. 15–16.
39 TCD, MS 5061, vol. 1, p. 22.
40 Ibid.
41 TCD, MS 5062, vol. 2, p. 16.
42 Eliot Warbourton, TCD, MS 5053, pp. 1–10.
43 See J. King, 'Mortuary Spectacles: The Genealogy of the Images of the Coffin Ships and Fever Sheds', in M. Corporaal, O. Frawley and E. Mark-FitzGerald (eds), *The Great Irish Famine: Visual and Material Cultures* (Liverpool: Liverpool University Press, forthcoming), pp. 88–109.
44 MacDonagh, *A Pattern of Government Growth*, pp. 185–7; Moran, *Sending Out Ireland's Poor*, pp. 101–16.
45 See King, 'Mortuary Spectacles', pp. 88–109.
46 TCD, MS 5075a/2 (1847), pp. 95–6.
47 Moran, *Sending Out Ireland's Poor*, p. 151.
48 TCD, MS 5075a/2 (1847), p. 118.
49 Ibid. pp. 155–6.
50 Ibid. p. 192.

51 TCD, MS 5073, p. 3; *British Canadian*, 20 May 1848, p. 1.
52 *Toronto Patriot*, 23 May 1848.
53 TCD, MS 5075a/2 (1847), pp. 175–6.
54 Ibid.
55 J. G. Jones, *The Abiding Enchantment of Curragh Chase: The Big House Remembered* (Cork: Clo Duanaire, 1983), p. 28.
56 Limerick City Archive, Aubrey De Vere Letters, P221/396.
57 TCD, MS 5061, vol. 1 (29 August–1 December 1847), p. 55.
58 Gray, 'Shovelling out your paupers', pp. 63–5; Moran, *Sending Out Ireland's Poor*, pp. 83–90.

Chapter Four

John Mitchel's Town, its Hinterland and the Great Famine

Anthony Russell

In 1848, John Mitchel (1815–75), a son of the Unitarian Manse in Newry and the most extreme of the Young Ireland rebels, was exiled to Van Diemen's Land, now Tasmania, for his seditious writing. In the 1860s, after supporting the reopening of the African slave trade and the American Confederacy, he was, for a short time, a leading Fenian. More than any other writer or politician, it was he who shaped the nationalist perception of the Great Famine when his ferocious pen declared that: 'The Almighty indeed sent the potato blight, but the English created the famine'.[1] As the consequences of potato blight spread, Mitchel was uncompromising in his condemnation of both the British Government's relief schemes and the man charged with their implementation, Charles Trevelyan, the Permanent Secretary to the Treasury. Mitchel referred to the 'harpy claw' in the dishes of children; to the Irish beholding 'their own wretched food melting in rottenness ... to heavy leaden ships, freighted with yellow corn their own hands have sown and reaped, spreading all sail for England'.[2] In February 1847, commenting on the destitution he witnessed, Mitchel memorably blamed Trevelyan:

> I could see, in front of the cottages, little children leaning against a fence when the sun shone out for they could not stand, their limbs fleshless, their bodies half-naked, their faces bloated yet wrinkled, and of a pale, greenish hue ... I saw Trevelyan's claw in the vitals of those children: his red tape would draw them to death: in his Government laboratory he had prepared for them the typhus poison.[3]

Mitchel thought the Great Famine was used as an excuse for mass murder. He wrote, 'A million and a half men women and children were carefully, prudently and peacefully slain by the British Government. They died in hunger in the midst of abundance, which their own hands had created'.[4] From Mitchel's perspective, British policy was designed with the intention of ridding Ireland of its surplus poor and 'shaking small lease-holders from the soil'.[5] James S. Donnelly has pointed out that Mitchel's accusation of murder and his powerful indictment of British policy during the Great Famine, 'was not answered'[6] until the revisionism of the 1960s when, because of his vehement language, the extremity of his accusations[7] and especially his support of slavery, Mitchel 'became a bête noir for many historians'.[8] However, in 2012, despite the efforts of revisionists 'to exorcise the ghost of nationalism from historical discourse',[9] Tim Pat's Coogan's book, *The Famine Plot*, reignited an interest and belief in 'Mitchel's enormously effective propaganda'.[10] In measured contrast, Brendan O'Cathair had suggested that Mitchel's 'inflamed mind mistook the combination of laissez-faire economic dogma, parsimony, inefficiency and insensitivity for genocide'.[11]

Whether one agrees with Mitchel's view on culpability or not, his descriptions of terminal destitution were penned not about the landscape surrounding Mitchel's home town, Newry, but rather they followed an electioneering visit in support of Young Ireland to Galway in 1847. Mitchel's emotive famine writing was, therefore, arguably not explicitly about his native Ulster; nor about Newry and the surrounding counties, Down, Louth and Armagh. How then did Newry, the location of the 2015 National Famine Commemoration, and its hinterland fare during the Great Famine?

Christine Kinealy, in challenging the once commonly held view that 'the north of Ireland did not experience the same catastrophy as did the rest of the country',[12] challenged writers to follow Gerard Mac Atasney's 'ground breaking study of the Famine in Lurgan and Portadown'[13] and to engage with local sources. Following on from research carried out for Newry and Mourne District Council's 1997 multimedia exhibition, 'The Great Famine in Newry and Mourne', this chapter focuses on the experience of Mitchel's town, south Down, north Louth and south Armagh during the Great Famine (*An Gorta Mór*). In so doing it will suggest that the Great Famine was a geographical famine, a social famine but not an ethnic famine.

Pre-Famine: South Down, South Armagh and North Louth

Pre-Famine, most of the land in Ireland was occupied by tenants-at-will. Unlike the rest of Ireland, east Ulster's farmers enjoyed Tenant Right: not a lease but an unwritten agreement that allowed a departing, even an evicted tenant, to have the value of any improvements he had made, and to sell his tenancy to someone else – provided, of course, it was someone of whom the landlord, or his agent, approved. For example, in March 1844, John Trainor, a linen trader from Green Island, Warrenpoint Road, Newry, claimed he was evicted from his eleven and a half acres on the Commons townland for voting for Denis Caufield Brady, a Liberal. John Trainor had found another person willing to pay him £150 for his tenancy. His complaint was not that he was evicted – he expected that – but that he had to settle for Lord Kilmorey's choice of tenant and a mere £60 to cover the cost of his 'ejectment'. However, Trainor did admit that he was offered another tenancy elsewhere and Kilmorey's agent, Thomas Gibson Henry, pointed out that since the Borough of Newry enjoyed the 'elective franchise' around Newry town he would only allow Presbyterian tenants. Thomas Gibson Henry claimed Trainor's case was the exception and that, 'upon the rest of the estate there is no reference to a man's religion or politics'.[14] In addition to Tenant Right farmers, more so than in the rest of Ireland, cottage-based spinners and weavers of flax into linen occupied many small tenancies, especially in a 'Linen Triangle' from Newry to Dungannon to Belfast, and along the Flurry River valley, in Ravensdale, between Newry and Dundalk.[15]

At the base of the pre-Famine social hierarchy, cottiers and labourers were employed by the larger tenant farmers. Cottiers had an agreement with the tenant farmer who supplied him with a cabin and a potato garden. The cottier had a certain unwritten security. Labourers were casual and relied on 'conacre' – renting a small area of land to grow potatoes in return for their labour or, sometimes, cash. If they did not succeed in renting land they queued in market squares hoping for short-term employment.

In July 1845, a correspondent for the *Belfast Penny Journal* identified the vertical dichotomy between the better-off tenant farmers and cottiers and labourers. He described County Down as 'the best conditioned quarter of Ireland', but commented: 'Many of the dwellings I saw upon the road looked to me like the abodes of extinguished hope ... grovelling, despairing almost idiotic wretchedness. I did not know that men and women, upright and made in the likeness of God could live in styes, like swine, with swine'.[16]

This skewed perception of the potato economy did not recognise that, in the absence of pasture, feeding potato skins and refuse to a pig was a way of gaining some cash; that for cottiers and labourers, 'their pig and manure heap constitute their only property'.[17] The pig was an asset that needed to be taken in at night. However, the hovel identified by the *Penny Journal* was an example of fourth-class housing, a single-roomed mud-walled cabin, and in 1841, as Table 1 shows, they represented between 12 per cent and 42 per cent of the housing in the baronies around Newry.[18]

Thus even in County Down, 'the garden of Ireland',[19] one-fifth of the housing consisted of mud cabins which were 'seldom a protection against the weather'.[20] The percentage was even higher in densely populated south Armagh, where the land is more mountainous.

Although Mitchel agreed with O'Connell that the 1843–45 Devon Commission into the occupation of land was 'a jury of butchers trying a sheep for its life',[21] it and the earlier 1833–34 *Commission to Enquire into the Conditions of the Poorer Classes in Ireland* both provided detailed descriptions of the social conditions and economy of rural Ireland, including Newry and district. Witnesses to the Devon Commission – better-off farmers, clergymen and land agents – gave evidence suggesting farm size around Newry was seven acres. This was a significant number for the commission, since it was the number it identified for holdings being 'inadequate to support the families residing upon them.' In Ireland there were 326,084 farms of seven acres or fewer.[22]

Table 1. The percentage of fourth-class housing in baronies around Newry, 1841

Barony	Fourth-class Housing	County
Upper Fews	31%	South Armagh
Upper Orier	42%	East Armagh
Lower Orier	18%	South Armagh
Newry	12%	South Down
Upper Iveagh	24%	South Down
Mourne	20%	South Down

Three Church of Ireland clergymen from Clonallan Parish, south of Newry in County Down, described housing conditions to the earlier 1833–4 Commission: 'The cabins of the poorer classes are generally of clay, roofed with sods and thatch ... The bedsteads are mostly filled with straw and frequently their only covering is the clothes they wear during the day.'[23] In evidence to the Devon Commission, Downshire's agent, Thomas Gibson Henry, emphasized the social condition and isolation of labourers when he commented: 'There are labourers, but I know nothing of them, as they do not come under my cognisance. They hold under tenants … who set them houses and perhaps a garden.'[24] George William Bradell, an agent, stated that in Clonduff, to the east of Newry, farm size ranged from three to thirty acres, that there was frequent use of usurers to pay the rent and that many relied on money from children who had already emigrated to England, but both large and small farmers were improving.[25]

The Revd James Porter, a Presbyterian minister from Drumlee, County Down, gave evidence to the Devon Commission on 18 March 1844 about the barony of Upper Iveagh. It stretched from near Newry in the west to Castlewellan in the east, from Banbridge in the north to Rostrevor in the south. He answered the Commission's questions as follows:

What is the extent of the district with which you consider yourself acquainted?

I think I am acquainted with the whole barony of Upper Iveagh.

Is it very populous?

Remarkably dense, the population.

What is the state of agriculture generally, is it improving or otherwise?

Decidedly improving.

Can you give the average of the size of farms?

I can give you an accurate one. There are 5,671 farms; this will give an average, of seven acres, three roods and one perch.

What is the usual mode of culture followed there?

In small farms, the spade is ... used; but almost throughout the whole of the district ploughing.

> **What is the usual rent of average land of different qualities?**
>
> On lands not so favourably situated, our rents are £2 2s; but they are all paupers; many of the houses are unrooted.
>
> **Under what class do labourers usually hold their cottages and by whom are they built and repaired?**
>
> By the farmers: the farmers have some cottiers' houses upon their farms usually.
>
> **What is the usual tenure by which the labourers hold their cottages?**
>
> From year to year.[26]

The Revd Porter's evidence, from the heart of County Down, tells of improvement and average farm size being over the significant seven acres, but he also describes a clear social dichotomy. Cottiers and labourers live in 'unrooted houses,' presumably fourth-class cabins. They used the spade, not the plough, and had the insecurity of not knowing if they would be employed the following year.

In Donaghmore parish, County Down, to the north of Newry, James Harshaw, a Presbyterian farmer of eighty acres and author of the 'Harshaw Diaries', reported increasing population and severe subdivision of holdings, with the majority under fifteen acres. The larger farms, like his own, practised a five- or six-year rotation with fertiliser and were therefore not dependent upon the potato. When asked about the smaller tenantry, he replied, 'I think their comforts are not improving'. He thought the condition of the labourers had changed little.[27]

In his diaries from 1841 to 1867[28] (the entries at the start of the famine from 17 April 1845 to 1 February 1846 are missing), James Harshaw (1797–1867) gave a daily account of his working and family life. His eighty acres produced potatoes, flax, tow, oats, wheat, hay, honey, peas, carrots, white carrots, turnips, apples, firkins of butter, lambs, pigs, turf and even eels. He employed labourers and paid them in both cash and produce. On 3 June 1846, he refers to ten labourers: 'Six men sodding potatows on the near dambray. Fur men molding in the brirybray'.[29] He bought seed potatoes, livestock, Dutch flaxseed, lime, guano and clover seed. When ill he had his head bled by leeches.[30] With such a variety of produce, the failure of the 'potatow' would have a limited impact. Such evidence from County Down generally tells of prosperity and improvement but, as in Table 1, it also identifies a numerous, poor and insecure underclass of cottiers and labourers living in cabins.

Across the Clanrye River in South Armagh, the evidence given to the Devon Commission was not as optimistic. David Craig of Newtownhamilton, a farmer of forty acres, acknowledged Tenant Right but thought that it was 'diminishing' in value. He was involved in improving his own land but in evidence to the Commission he thought that the smaller tenantry lived in poverty and that the condition of the labourers bordered on pauperism.[31] The Revd Gunn Brown and the Revd West, both Presbyterian ministers, lamented the lack of improving landlords, the deteriorating conditions for all classes and difficulty in paying the rent:

> **What is your opinion of the condition of the smaller tenantry?**
>
> [Revd West] – They are worse again, a great deal. They have not the means to get on, so as to make the value of their land.
>
> **With respect to the class of labourers, does their condition seem to be improving?**
>
> [Revd West] – No, the average price of wage is getting every year less; the farmers cannot afford to give wages they formly gave.[32]

The Revd Gunn Brown claimed that even the larger farms were, 'now poorly dressed and no longer had a pig hanging in the chimney'.[33] The evidence of Revd Michael Lennon, Parish Priest of Upper Creegan, South Armagh, to the Devon Commission considered 'that the condition of the occupiers of small farms, in the district we speak of, has been gradually getting worse … the present condition is therefore most wretched and pitiable; Their little capital … is altogether gone, and they have scarcely any other resource; except applying to usurers'.[34] When asked about the labourers, he replied: 'The condition of the labourers is still, [if] possible, worse … the farmers are not able to give them the accustomed employment'.[35] The Revd Lennon stated that the labourers paid for their cabins and potato garden with their labour. There were no large farms in his area[36] but:

> [T]he general run of farms is very small … the general average is from five to twenty acres, and the greater number of them is under ten: and in the district of Forkhill and Killevy, the greater number is under five

> acres. It is not by farming the people live but by dealing: they look upon their holdings, or little farms, as rather a lodging or resting place. They go to England to labour: and many of them purchase various articles, and go through the country with them.[37]

Plurality of income has a long history in South Armagh, but around Omeath, north County Louth, there were also cadgers, selling fish in local towns and even in Belfast. There were pahvees, from north Louth and South Armagh, who sold locally produced cloth,[38] some of which was produced by the weaver-crofters of the Ravensdale valley. Their 'journeys' were undertaken when the potato was in the ground.[39]

In parts of South Armagh and above Omeath, north Louth, the rundale system, with its associated communal clachans, had survived. In evidence to the Devon Commission in 1845, the Revd Lennon referred to five or six families all living in the same street: 'They had their fields a little way off'.[40] Landlords viewed clachans as an inefficent use of land and preferred dispersed farmsteads, with the tenant living on the land he was farming. They set about reorganising the landscape, creating more efficient economic units like the ladder farms still evident on the slopes of Slieve Gullion and Camlough Mountain. In Ballymacdermot townland, on the eastern slopes of Camlough, the landlord created five-acre farms stretching from a lowland bog to the side of the mountain.[41] The Revd Lennon described consolidation, 'lines drawn across the entire townland and everyman gets his lot by itself'.[42] Pre-Famine, clachans also survived above Omeath in Ardagy and on the better-drained glacial deposits along the Glemmore Valley, where increasing population pressure had caused many people to move.[43]

The bitterness created in the transition from rural nucleation to dispersal survived in the folk memory. Mary Daly from Crossmaglen, born in 1874, recalled:

> I mind them telling it many a time that they got threepence a day to pull down their own houses at Cross and build them into ditches. Old Barry McKenna used to tell it often that there was scores of houses fornint he's door around the time of the famine, but people was all thrown out, and got threepence a day to pull down their own houses.[44]

Thus the evidence given to the Devon Commission from the more mountainous South Armagh and its border with Louth described a lack of improvement and poverty, more so than in the rolling drumlins of County Down. However, the Revd Lennon did admit that Tenant Right 'is nearly universally admitted'.[45] This included his congregation in north Louth.

In evidence to the Devon Commission in Carlingford, north Louth, James O'Hanlon claimed that in townlands 'in which the landlord is resident the state of the tenantry is far superior to the others'. He too referred to the labourers holding 'a cottage with a garden attached' under 'farmers both large and small'. Their rent was usually paid 'in labour'.[46] In a 1950s study of the richer arable land on the Cooley Peninsula, south of Carlingford, T. Jones Hughes noted the 'ephemeral nature of cottier settlement'[47] and observed: 'Here as so often in East Leinster, the greatest wretchedness appeared on the richest land'.[48] This twentieth-century study echoes the observation of the *Belfast Penny Journal* in 1845 of a vulnerable underclass living beside, and below, wealthier tenant farmers. It was they who relied on the potato, which could be cultivated with a spade and did not require processing. Thus, when the *Newry Commercial Telegraph* recorded the arrival of the blight, *phytophthora infestans*, on 23 September 1845,[49] the disease was not only infecting potato fields and gardens but also the base of a rural social and economic hierarchy.

It was the smaller tenant, the cottier and the labourer, all evident in Newry's hinterland, who were most exposed. That they had no land, or rented only a few acres, and over the next five years were largely to disappear from the landscape proved, to Mitchel's hindsight, that the main aim of the Devon Commission was the consolidation of small farms and the removal of 196,368 families. Using the Great Famine as the means, British policies were responsible for the 'killing of a million persons'.[50]

The Great Famine in Newry and its Hinterland

In 1845, Newry was a relatively prosperous port anticipating the arrival of the railway and an enlarged ship canal. The 1844 *Parlimentary Gazetteer* noted exports of £616,836 and imports of £568,711, a healthy balance in favour of produce from the town and its hinterland. Due to the inland canal, the Newry Navigation, reaching to the River Bann and Lough Neagh, the sale of butter exceeded that of Belfast by upwards of 3,300 tons per annum. Exports included nearly 25,000 tons of cornmeal and flour, but despite being widely grown only 267 tons of potatoes were exported,[51] presumably an indication of their subsistence value.

The 1845 failure of the potato crop was partial in Ireland and around Newry. In County Down, one-quarter of the potato crop was lost, and in Armagh, one-fifth. On 13 November, Colonel Close, a landlord from Drumbanager with 9,087 acres, called a meeting in Poyntzpass, 'to take into consideration the awfully diseased state of the potato and the best alternative and remedy'. The meeting considered how to save the crop. Potatoes 'partially diseased, ought at least to produce 6lbs of dry starch, for which 1½d may ... be safely calculated upon'.[52] As yet there was no need to consider helping the poor, and at this time there were 322 inmates in Newry Workhouse,[53] well below its 1,000 capacity. The *Newry Commercial Telegraph*'s New Year message was optimistic: 'Eighteen hundred and forty-six has this day opened upon us ... hopeful for the continuance of our country's prosperity ... we cordially wish friends and foes ... a Happy New Year'. The optimism was reflected in Ballybot Market (the Armagh side of Newry) where higher horse prices could be attributed to 'The great increase in Labour on the different railways'.[54]

Across the river on the Down side of the town, however, Magistrate Singleton was writing to Dublin Castle about the market there. Geese had doubled in price, as had other foods, but with regard to the potato, 'it was melancholy to see so many cartloads totally unfit for human consumption for sale in a town of 12,000 inhabitants'.[55] On 30 May 1846, the minutes of the Board of Guardians for the Newry Union recorded, 'no tenders were received in answer to the advertisment for a contract for potatoes',[56] but on 5 June 1846, James Harshaw recorded in his diary: 'From John Martin 8cwt of potatows, from Master Brown 2cwt of seed potatows', having earlier on 3 June bought seed potatoes at Newry Market.[57] James Harshaw notes that on 14 June his minister, 'lactured from the parable of the rich man & Lazarus.' It was a partial and spatial failure of the potato.

Over the county border in South Armagh conditions were worse. The potato had generally failed and in Forkhill on 9 December 1845 a relief committee of resident landlords, clergymen and larger farmers was established.[58] It met in May 1846 to help the poor through the 'meal months', when traditionally the supply of potatoes was exhausted and the poor relied on 'a meagre diet of oatmeal and barley until they could harvest a new crop of potatoes ... by June 1846, £525 had been subscribed locally by landlords and clergymen.' They bought Indian meal, imported by the Peel Government, and sold it 'cheaply and on credit'.[59]

On 14 July 1846, the *Newry Commercial Telegraph* reported the second failure of the potato crop: 'We believe that every potato crop is affected'.[60]

On 20 August, the paper announced the end of Sir Robert Peel's scheme to import Indian corn and the setting up of public works under the new Prime Minister Lord John Russell's Labour Rate Act, 1847: 'There is to be no copying after the Peel school in respect of food consumption. Trafficking in Indian Corn will be left to the dealers ... Employment instead of rations of flour, is to be furnished for the masses. Public works on an extensive scale are to be initiated ... under the Board of Works'.[61] To this end, T.N. Redington, Dublin Castle, wrote to Joshua M. McGee, Newry, directing that an Extraordinary Presentment Session be convened for the Barony of Upper Orier.[62] Other baronies would follow suit.

However, despite this drastic action, and reflecting, as yet, any major impact of the potato failure in the Newry area, the *Telegraph* confidently proclaimed:

> There seems to be a dread of famine in the land. We do not participate in such feelings. No doubt, to the masses especially in country districts where the produce of the potato garden has formed the sole dependence of families much inconvenience and a certain amount of deprivation will be the consequence ... but starvation is not to be feared ... there is no risk of any Irishman starving to death.[63]

Presentment Sessions to organise Public Works were slow to initiate projects and in November 1846 only 107 people were employed in County Armagh and none in County Down.[64] However, there was increasing need as the consequences of the second potato crop failure became more obvious on the rural landscape and on the streets of Newry. The price of potatoes in Newry market, which had been 3d per stone in May 1844, trebled to 10d by 30 November 1846.[65] Perhaps good news for James Harshaw, who on 10 November 1846, recorded: 'a dark, dry day with south wind dug potatows & wheat, on the far long drils – ended the ploughing of Morgans field'.[66] Harshaw was still lifting potatoes in mid-December.

'Outrages' were beginning to happen. In early November, there was an attempt to rob the corn mill at 'Derrylecka' to the east of Newry.[67] In mid-November, 15 cwt of food was robbed from the smack *Eagle* at Carlingford. In Armagh, 'a number of labourers carrying spades and other implements entered the city and visited bakers' shops demanding food'.[68] By 9 January 1847, Newry Workhouse was full; designed for 1,000 inmates, it had 1,116 paupers and rising.[69] Dr Morrison, from the fever hospital on the Rathfriland

Road, Newry, reported that he had never known disease to be so prevalent and that some people were so desperate for food and shelter 'that there was not a day when someone did not apply to the fever hospital feigning fever and exposing himself to the disease'.[70] Around Forkhill, Lieutenant Griffith, Inspecting Officer, reported that the cottiers and labourers were close to starvation. He called for soup kitchens to be established, 'as the easiest and cheapest remedy to hand'.[71]

The *Newry Commercial Telegraph* was no longer complacent and on 12 December 1846, a correspondent proclaimed: 'The hand of divine Providence has been laid on our country and Newry has not been exempted'.[72] The local community also noticed and responded. On 18 December 1846, James Harshaw recorded the setting up of a relief committee in Loughorne, at the home of the Revd Quinn.[73] Following a private meeting to establish a soup kitchen on New Street, Newry, when Lord Kilmorey sent his apologies and £25, a public meeting was held. Dr Savage pointed out that a great number of the poor belonged to the same community as himself and did not eat meat on days forbidden by the Church. The Revd Baggot, the Church of Ireland minister, assured him that on Fridays there would be 'pea soup, well seasoned gruel and bread'. The sum of £500 was collected and the subscribers were given tickets to distribute to the poor. The charge was one penny per ticket.[74] This charge was later dropped because it was regarded as 'an incentive to mendicancy'.[75] Soup kitchens were also established at Warrenpoint and Kilkeel.[76]

During the harsh winter of 1847, the local Baronial Committees met and expressed sympathy with the poor but struggled to establish public works. In early January, the Baronial session for Upper Orier heard that two-thirds of the people were in a state of destitution.[77] In County Armagh, 3,077 were employed in public works; in Down the figure was 280. In contrast, the figure for Cavan was 23,468.[78] For Upper Orier, it was suggested that the railways offered the best hope of employment. It was pointed out that Mr Dargan, the railway engineer, already had full employment and a voice from the floor proclaimed that 'the poor could not stand the work'.[79] Mr Benson, a landowner from Fathom, agreed. He stated that there were a number of people in his townlands, Upper and Lower Fathom, 'in a state of starvation and could not go a distance to work on the railway. Besides if they should leave home to get work for themselves what would their wives and families do?' Benson claimed £50, for the purpose of cutting a 'hill on the road leading from the Wellington Inn on the Dublin Road to Fatham'.[80]

To his credit, during January and February 1847, Benson did establish 'soup boilers from which to issue about quarts of soup'. In a letter to Sir Randolph Routh, Dublin Castle, Benson claimed that besides providing food he also distrubuted medicines to 'a great number of poor People'.[81] However, the folk memory was not kind to Benson. Sarah Grant from Jonesborough, born in 1860, told the Irish Folklore Commission in 1945: 'If you'd take Benson's gravy they'd have a claim on you and you'd have to send the children to the Protestant school at Adavoyle'.[82] Charges of souperism, like this one, survive in the folk memory aound Forkhill.

John Martin, Young Irelander, nephew of the diarist James Harshaw, and John Mitchel's best friend, was a small landlord in County Down. He thought: 'The resident landlords of Ireland, with scarcley an exception are engaged, each in the locality for which he is especially interested, in endeavouring to alleviate the heavy distress spread over our unhappy island'.[83] John Mitchel had already warned his friend against offering too much help to his tenants: 'I will not torment you further on the matter. Only remember that by trying to do more than there are means to do a man may suddenly deprive himself of the power to do anything at all'.[84]

Captain Brereton, the Board of Works Inspecting Officer, would not have agreed with John Martin that resident landlords were keen to provide aid. On 9 January, at Castlewellan, with 6,000 'famishing people' outside, he was attacked by landlords 'for bringing the destitution of the barony (Mourne) before their notice'. Despite reporting 'upwards of 2,000 families destitute', Brereton recorded 'a great desire evinced by the landed proprietors to hide the poverty of the people'[85] and very great distress in Rathfriland, Ballymacarret and the Mournes. In Kilkeel, he recorded 300 destitute men waiting for employment from the Committee and feared, 'their destitution is such that nothing but instant relief, by employment, can keep them from committing some flagrant outrage'.[86] On 13 February, in his journal, he again referred to Rathfriland and condemned the agent of the absentee landlord, General Meade, for giving 'sparingly to his famishing tenantry'.[87] Meade's agent had claimed in November that a rent abatement had been made on the condition that 'Chief tenants having cottiers will afford them as much employment as possible in improvements on their farms'.[88] Brereton highlighed the failure of Public Works. With a population of 22,000 in the Mourne Barony, a third were in 'utter destitution ... and the funds of the Committee are utterly inadequate to administer relief to the wants of this fast increasing misery'.[89] Earlier, on 9 January 1847, James Harshaw was, ironically, both giving out relief tickets to the poor and 'digging potatows in Bettys upperfield'.[90]

In Armagh, on 6 February 1847, the distinction between the larger farmers and the smaller tenants, cottiers and labourers was also apparent to the Inspecting Officer for the county. On one level, he reported normality: 'In the Barony of Armagh ploughing has commenced pretty generally, and the other ordinary farm operations appear in the state of progress'. However, in the smaller holdings, he observes, 'there is as yet very little labour', and he described 'the destitution of the people' in the baronies of Upper Orier, Upper Fews and Armagh.[91] Public works were hard to sustain and 'In January 1847, the Forkhill Relief Committee complained that only one-tenth of the district's 1,220 labourers were employed' on schemes.[92] The *Newry Commercial Telegraph*'s adverts recorded one type of work: 'The labouring poor are now employed in breaking stones which were available for farmers to buy'. Thus the evidence from Newry's hinterland, in both Down and Armagh, tells of the juxtoposition of agricurtural normality and destitution.

In the Ravensdale valley and 'the north of Ireland ... where it was the practice for the small farmer to combine weaving and spinning with his agriculture profession',[93] the crofter-weavers were also becoming destitute. As Belfast rapidly developed, they were already suffering from competition from the mechanisation and urbanisation of the linen industry. Prices for linen were so low that weaving families in the parish of Tartaraghan, County Armagh, were 'sitting up three nights a week in order by any means to procure food for their families'.[94] Following the failure of the potato crop, the supply of turnips, 'on which numbers were subsisting' was exhausted.[95] Mainly Presbyterians, they sold or pawned their clothes and even their Bibles. This evidence from a Quaker continued:

> I have myself witnessed the living lying on straw, by the side of the unburied dead, who had died three days before. Many cases of deaths from actual starvation have occurred amongst the able-bodied, without reckoning the aged and the infirm … or the very many children who have died from the same cause. I have called to see a girl of four years old, a few weeks ago a strong healthy girl, who was so emaciated as to be unable to either stand or move a limb. I have visited houses where there was no article whatever of food or clothing, nothing but straw to lie down upon, not even a stool to sit on, – some of whose inmates I fear must have perished.[96]

Such scenes are similar to those described by John Mitchel as he travelled to Galway, but this was Ulster, near Loughall, where the Orange Order was founded.

The hungry moved towards the towns seeking food. On 2 Janauary 1847, 'a multitude of poor looking men and boys ... many of them smallholders' went to Markethill, entered many shops and took loaves.[97] They signed a petition and went home. On 6 January 1847, opposite Warrenpoint, the schooner *Lively* was boarded, the captain and the crew trapped below decks, and several bags of oatmeal were carried away.[98] On 14 January, the *Newry Commercial Telegraph*, in a rare moment of agreement with John Mitchel, claimed: 'In this town at present there are ... 10,000 barrels of flour held on speculation ... of advancing prices'.[99] This in a town where Captain Brereton, on 23 January 1847, reported that, 'the amount of misery in the town portion of the Barony ... arising out of scarity of food and want of employment is now perfectly frightful'. Across the barony, 800 families were destitute. Brereton praised the New Street Soup Kitchen Committee for feeding 1,100 people and concluded that if it had not been for such efforts, 'the destitution in the town would have been much worse'.[100]

Soup Kitchens and the Workhouse

The Government now agreed. Following the success of voluntary soup kitchens like Newry's, and the failure of public works, the Temporary Relief Act, February 1847, established soup kitchens across the country. Committees were reconstituted and voluntary work continued. The inaugural meeting of the Newry Ladies Benevolent Society was held on 17 February 1847,[101] during which they organised a bazaar to raise funds. On 20 March 1847, Mr N. Thompson, the Chairman of the Newry Relief Committee, could certify that the ladies of the Charitable Ladies Society of Newry had collected £157 7s, 'of which £97 7s had already been expended in giving gratuitous relief in food, clothing & straw to the poor of the Town & neighbourhood'. Thompson continued, 'I think it necessary to add that the ladies who manage this Society are Roman Catholics and that those receiving aid are also with some exceptions of that persuasion'.[102] Mrs Margaret Russell, who was chair of the Charitable Ladies of Newry Society, was the mother of the future Lord Charles Russell of Killowen, who would defend Parnell and become the first Catholic Lord Chief Justice of England since the Reformation. In March 1847, a meeting of young men involved in mercantile establishments set up a committee to relieve the poor and the destitute of Newry.[103]

Throughout January, the workhouse in Newry was full. In the week following 19 February, forty-two died there, and on 26 February, the master died. The matron, the schoolmaster and the acting schoolmaster were all sick with fever. Dr Davis also caught the fever, but on 27 March, the *Newry Commercial Telegraph* was able to report his convalesence.[104] The other officers died. Graph One shows the combined numbers treated at Newry Fever Hospital and in its dispensary from 1845 to 1850 as 3,977.[105] As elsewhere, 1847 is clearly the worst year of the Famine.

Migrants continued to move into Newry. 'Within the last three months what multitudes of paupers from the country have swarmed into Newry'. The *Newry Commercial Telegraph* complained that beggars infected 'the leading thoroughfares and besiege every door'. It suspected many were from Connaught and Munster and objected 'to supporting hordes of alien paupers'.[106]

Graph One
Newry Fever Hospital
Numbers treated

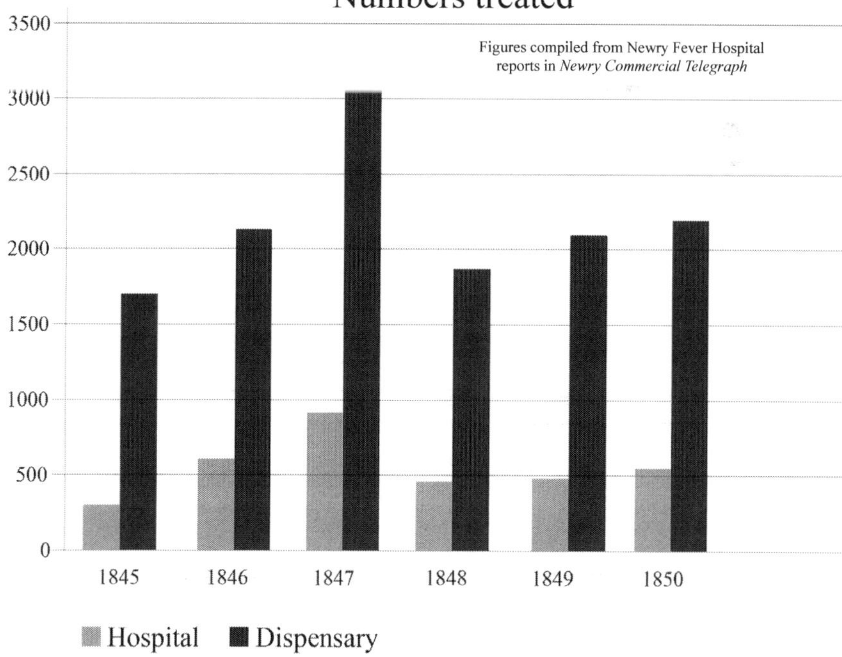

In April, Public Works ended and the Baronial Committees were replacd by local Relief Committees. On 5 April, James Harshaw noted the change in his diary: 'Attended the Relief Committee where Captain Glascock reconstituted it by Act of Parliament'.[107] At its inaugural meeting on 2 April, the Newry Committee, echoing the *Telegraph*'s opposition to feeding migrants, passed two resolutions:

1. That no person be put on the lists who has not been resident within the electoral division of Newry for the last four months.
2. That no person be placed on the destitute list, for gratuitous relief, as long as there is room in the poor house.[108]

News of distress around Newry crossed the Atlantic and on 11 May 1847 the American Society of Friends Irish Relief Committee wrote to their Dublin Central Relief Committee: 'We would like to call attention, as to the distinction of this shipment, to the locality of Newry; and if in your opinion it would do most good in that district, to direct a portion or all to that point.' However, Newry was not such a high priority for the Society of Friends. The transactions of their Central Committee show that in 1847 out of a total of £42,673 17s 6d only one cargo with a value of £42 8s 9d came to Newry, aboard the *Sea Nymph*.[109]

Conditions improved during the summer and the potato harvest was sound, but in Down and Armagh, 'multitudes of acres' were 'lying wholly or partially neglected' with 'small farmers destitute of the means to produce seed and manure'.[110] As a result, the harvest was too small to prevent famine conditions extending into 1848. Matters were made worse after the 1847 Poor Law Extension Act stopped gratuitous relief and the full burden of relief fell on the Poor Law Unions – the workhouses. For the first time, outdoor relief was allowed and the Newry Board of Guardians established eight relief districts each with a relieving officer.

The change in the law had a dramatic effect on Newry Workhouse. With the arrival of winter the numbers rose from 888 on 30 October 1847 to 3,945 in April 1848, including 2,998 on outdoor relief.[111] To cope with the numbers, in February 1848, an auxillary workhouse was opened on Canal Quay. With the exception of the winter of 1846–47, women outnumbered men by two to one in Newry Workhouse. Men could get work more easily – or they abandoned their wives and families and emigrated to America. On North Street Newry, the wife of one such person, who was abandoned in

1848, was two years later living in 'a wretched state of filfth' with her three youngest childen who were 'naked' and 'reduced to mere skeletons'. Even then she refused 'to come into [the] Workhouse'. On 22 November 1847, there were 518 children in the workhouse,[112] whereas a year earlier there were only twenty-nine children – a rise from 4 per cent to 60 per cent. Whole families were abandoning the land. The *Newry Commercial Telegraph* suggested that 28 per cent of the inmates were Protestants.[113]

The Newry Union participated in the Earl Grey scheme, which sent young women from poor backgrounds to Australia to try and correct the gender imbalance in the colonies. In May 1848, the minutes of the Board of Guardians record the master selecting eleven female paupers, and noting that 'only girls of unblemished character were selected'. On 15 July, the *Newry Examiner and Louth Advertiser* reported the young female inmates passing through Newry bound for Australia: 'They were all neatly clad, interesting looking girls, and appeared in the best of health and spirits'.[114] In the event, ten emigrated and a year later it was reported that they had arrived safely. 'The whole party, including 10 from Newry have met with situations ... at wages from £5–£10 per annum'.[115]

It was not only the onset of winter that drove people into the workhouse. The early signs for the potato crop were good but on 17 August it was reported from Rathfriland, 'the disease is here in all its virulence'.[116] This time the fungus attacked James Harshaw's crop in Loughorne. On 7 August 1848, he wrote: 'Desease first appeared in the potato tops on the footridge of the brirbray'.[117] Indicative of the distinction between the small tenant and large farmer, the failure of his potato crop did not stop James Harshaw, with his labourers, celebrating the harvest on 17 September 1848: 'The Dandy (his wife) gave the workers and some other gels and boys the "churn" ... John played the fiddle until one and they danced merrily'.[118]

(John Mitchel had been exiled in May and on 11 July 1848 James Harshaw noted the arrest of John Martin.)

Emigration and Cholera

As elsewhere in Ireland, around Newry, emigration was taking place at an alarming rate. 'Here too it is the industrious, thrifty class that is being drained. Day after day there are to be seen passing through the major thoroughfare, on the way to Warrenpoint, carts upon which are seated, on those high boxes betokening a sea voyage in prospect, young and hale looking men and

Graph Two
Emigration from Newry to New York
1846–1851

Total number of passengers 5,485

Source: I.A. Glazier, *The Famine Immigrants: Lists of Irish Immigrants Arriving at New York, 1841–1851*, vol. 7, part 1 (New York: Clearfield, 1986).

women', wrote the *Newry Commercial Telegraph*. Warrenpoint was Newry's outport and the emigrants were not leaving 'the wretched garret or cellar or cabin ... but ... the once comfortable habitation of the tradesman and cottage of the small farmer'.[119] Thus the *Telegraph* observed the impact of famine moving up the social scale. An analysis of seven ships that left Warrenpoint for New York from 1847 to 1849 supported the view that the emigrants were young. It found the average age to be twenty-six for males and twenty-three for females. They were overwhelmingly from an agricultural background, with 32 per cent labourers, 21 per cent farmers and 4 per cent ploughmen. Forty-three per cent were females, 39 per cent were males and 18 per cent were children.[120]

Graph Two shows that from 1846 to 1851 the total number of emigrants from Newry direct to New York was 5,485. This number does not include those who sailed from Newry to Liverpool and then on to New York. Newry's direct emigration to New York was 196 in 1846, reaching a peak of 1,716 in 1849 and then falling back to 378 in 1851. It made up less than 1 per cent of Irish emigration to New York.[121] Two of the emigrants out of Warrenpoint were the sons of the diarist James Harshaw, who both arrived in New York in good health on 18 December 1949 after a journey of sixty-five days on the bark *Janet*.[122]

A report to Parliament for 1847–8 concerning emigration to Canada recorded five ships and 1,488 passengers sailing to Quebec from the port of Newry during the 1847 sailing season. Out of the 1,488 passengers, 21 died on board, a death rate of 1.4 per cent.[123] This compares favourably with an estimated 16 per cent death rate for Irish emigrants to British North America.[124] From 1834, chain migration – where the first settlers tell of their success and encourage relatives to join them – was a feature of emigration from Cooley to Lower Cove, St John, New Brunswick. So much so that residents of that neighbourhood were known as 'coolies'.[125] In 1847, two ships from Newry arrived in St John, the *Sea Bird* (346 passengers) on 22 May and the *Lady Caroline* (105 passengers) on 23 July. No deaths were recorded.[126]

It was Thomas D'Arcy McGee, a Young Irelander born in Carlingford, who coined the term 'sailing coffins', but the ships leaving Newry, as illustrated above, were clearly not coffin ships. However, during the famine period three ships from Newry were lost: the *Hannah*, lost 29 April 1849, the *Ayrshire*, lost 13 January 1850 and the *Seraphine*, lost 25 May 1850. Only the *Hannah*, which hit an iceberg, had more than one fatality. The *Hannah*'s passengers, mainly 'agricultural labourers and their wives and children', tried to scamble onto the ice. One hundred and twenty-nine were rescued by the *Nicarque* but 'those who perished by being crushed between the ice and frozen to death were from fifty to sixty'.[127] Although she sailed from Carlingford Lough, the *Hannah* was not a Newry registered ship and the *Newry Commercial Telegraph* strongly advised emigrants to use a local port. With reference to Francis Carville's six ships, bound for Quebec and New York, the paper pointed out 'that during the last two years, when almost every passenger vessel to America from English ports, was more or less little better than a lazaretto, no sickness of a pestilential nature, took place on board his ships nor were any of the passengers by them obliged to be sent to Grosse Island'.[128]

Newry's ship owners and their agents were proud of their record and the papers carried letters from grateful passengers, but they and the keepers of lodgings, public houses and shops did well out of trade generated by famine. Like Carville, most of them were Catholics. A port like Newry/Warrenpoint, where those in the back streets lived 'amidst poisonous effluvia of every kind',[129] was vulnerable to cholera and the disease claimed its first victim in the Newry Bridewell, Kilmorey Street, on 20 February 1849.[130] It quickly spread to neighbouring streets and by the following

June there were 126 cases with 51 fatalities. In Killeavy, Jonesborough, Mullaghglass, Camlough and Rathfriland there were also twenty-two cholera deaths reported.[131]

Rate in Aid and Famine Ending

On 17 March 1849 there were 1,391 inmates in Newry Workhouse and 2,311 on outdoor relief.[132] Dealing with such numbers and overcrowding helped the Newry Guardians to react angrily to the Rate in Aid Bill, 'imposed on every poor law union in the country in the aid of twenty three bankrupt unions, all of them with the exception of Glenties (County Donegal) in the provinces of Connacht and Munster'.[133] On 24 February 1849, the Guardians passed a resolution, proposed by Colonel Close, which ended: 'we emphatically deny that the industrious population of the province are under any moral obligation to sustain the burden of poverty of any other province of Ireland'.[134] In the *Newry Commercial Telegraph*, a letter from *Agricola* suggested Rate in Aid 'would reduce the sturdy, spirited independent Yeomanry of Ulster to the loathesome degraded conditions of the Connaught pauper'.[135] Of course, the cottiers and labourers of Down and Armagh were an underclass and not independent yeomen. Despite their opposition, the Newry Guardians did finish paying the rate of 'upwards of £3000' on 12 January 1850.[136]

In 1849, conditions around Newry were improving, and Graph Three shows a dramatic fall in the numbers both in the workhouse and on outdoor relief, suggesting that the famine was ending earlier around Newry.

One reason for the fall in numbers seeking relief was Mr Dargan's rush to complete both the Warrenpoint to Newry railway line and the Albert Basin on the new ship canal. Employment on canal work rose from 400 in July to 2,000 at the end of August.[137] Railway and canal work was blamed for bringing Ribbonism and violence to the Newry area. 'At and around Fathom ... and even on the Co. Down side symptons of the ribbon spirit manifest themselves.' The *Newry Commercial Telegraph* further complained, 'since our peaceful community has been invaded by railway workers, most of whom belong to other parts of Ireland, there have been so many outrages committed that they merely call upon transient feelings of astonishment'.[138]

The potato crop around Newry did not fail. In Newry Market 'an old favourite the potato is in great abundance'.[139] Throughout the year the price

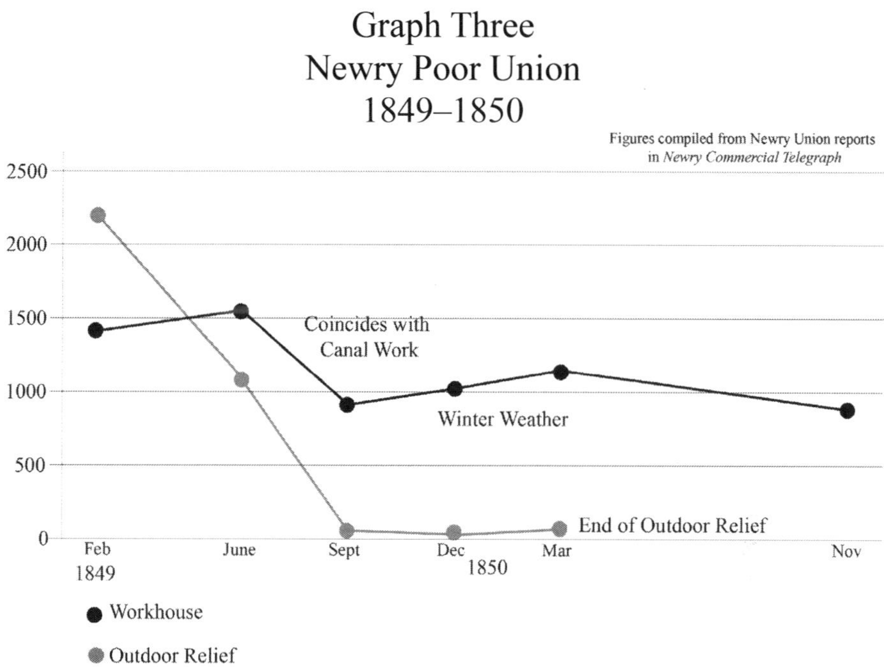

of potaoes fell in Newry market and on 18 September they were at the pre-famine price of 3d per stone.[140] On 9 September 1849, the Newry Workhouse was below capacity, with 854 immates and another 90 on outdoor relief.[141] On 3 November, the figure was 815, with 'the number employed much greater than the number of able bodied paupers'.[142] The unusually cold winter of 1849–50 pushed the numbers in the workhouse back up to 1,364, most of whom were 'able bodied men and women who stated they could not obtain work due to the inclement weather'.[143] On 30 March 1850, the numbers were back to 1,066, with 66 on outdoor relief. In the house, 53 per cent were boys, girls and infants, 34 per cent were adult females; 4 per cent were aged or infirm adult males. Only 9 per cent were able-bodied adult males, suggesting work was available.[144]

Whilst 1849 brought a measure of recovery to Newry, a letter on 17 March to the *Newry Commercial Telegraph* from Louisberg Glebe, Westport read: 'The famine years of 1846, 1847, and 1848 were halcyon days when contrasted with this dismal year 1849! ... the sandbanks about me are studded with the bodies of the dead'.[145] The famine clearly continued unabated in the west.

The Statistical Impact of the Famine in Newry and its Hinterland

On average, in the seventy-five townlands surrounding Newry there was a 17 per cent loss of population in the census figures between 1841 and 1851. However, there was great variation between townlands – some lost population while others gained.

Map One shows the differences in population beween 1841 and 1851 in the townlands closest to the town.[146] The more mountainous area to the south-west of the town, part of South Armagh, suffered the highest losses, including the mainly Presbyterian townland of Altnaveigh, which lost 30 per cent of its population. Townlands to the south of the town, like Lower Fathom, which gained less than 1 per cent, had a tradition of work associated with shipping and the port. Townlands around the town, like Lisdrumgullion,

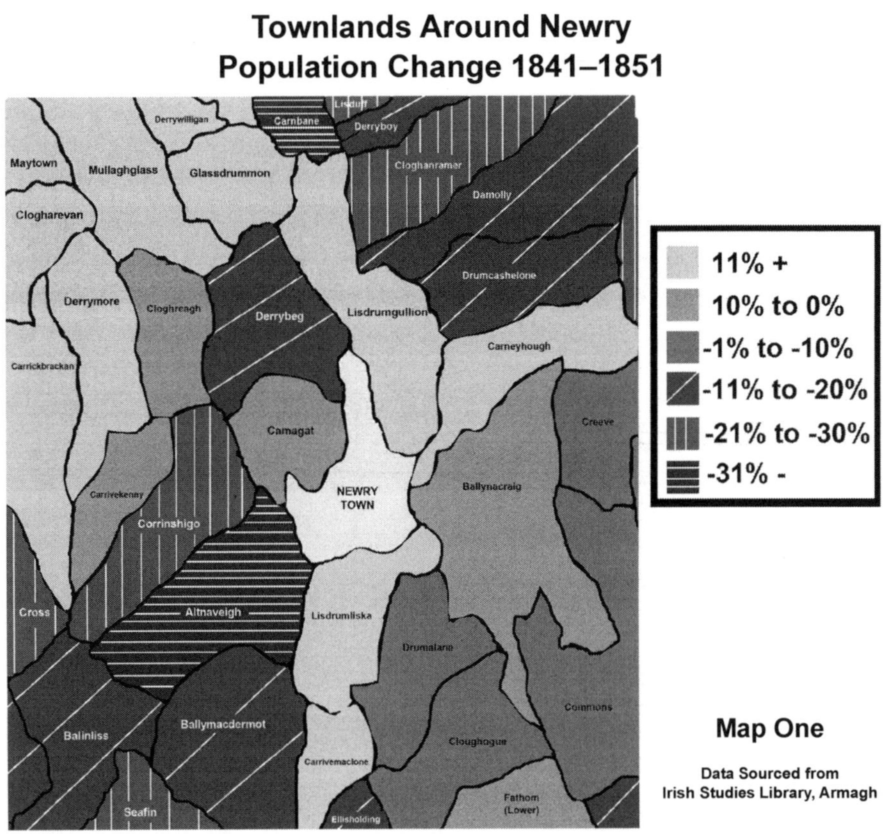

Map One

Data Sourced from Irish Studies Library, Armagh

Baronies around Newry
Population Loss 1841–1851

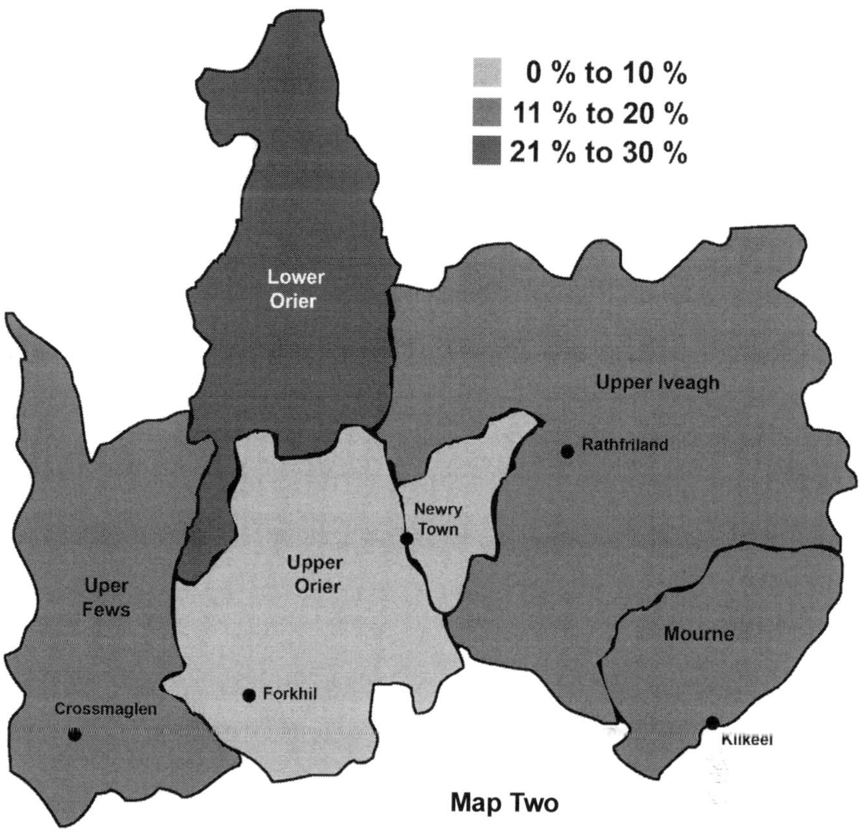

Map Two

Data sourced from
Irish Studies Library, Armagh

which gained 47 per cent, may have reflected the rural to urban migration and work associated with the town, like carting, including moving coal from the canal docks to the gasworks on Kilmorey Street. Those townlands to the north-west, like Mullaghglass, which gained 31 per cent, are associated with railway building, quarries and mills. However, the County Down townlands to the north-east lost significant population between 1841 and 1851. Cottiers, labourers and small tenants were vulnerable no matter how prosperous the townland they were in. At local level, as well as at national level, geography mattered.

Table 2. Percentages of fourth-class housing in baronies around Newry, 1841 and 1851

Barony	**Fourth-class Housing, 1841**	**Fourth-class Housing, 1851**	**County**
Upper Fews	31%	8%	South Armagh
Upper Orier	42%	11%	South Armagh
Lower Orier	18%	7%	East Armagh
Newry	12%	2%	South Down
Upper Iveagh	24%	7%	South Down
Mourne	20%	4%	South Down

Moving out from Newry town and its immediate townlands, Map Two shows that the baronies around Newry lost significant numbers between 1841 and 1851 but they did not, on average, suffer a loss of population on the same scale as the west and south-west of Ireland.

Ballybot, the Armagh portion of Newry town, with rural to urban migration, the workhouse and the canal and railway building, may have distorted and reduced the figure for Upper Orier. Table 2 shows the severe reduction in fourth-class housing in the baronies around Newry between 1841 and 1851, regardless of pre-famine prosperity or otherwise.[147]

Given that this was the housing of the small tenant farmer, cottier and labourer it was they who bore the brunt of the famine. For example, in the County Down parish of Donaghmore, mainly in Upper Iveagh, fourth-class housing fell from 199 in 1841 to 16 in 1851, whilst first- and second-class housing rose from 232 to 289. The population of the parish fell from 4,436 in 1841 to 3,434 in 1851, a loss of 22 per cent from a relatively prosperous parish,[148] but the housing data suggest it was the small tenant, the cottier and the labourer who suffered most.

In the County Armagh parish of Forkhill, in Upper Orier, fourth-class housing fell from 795 in 1841 to 142 in 1851, whilst first- and second-class housing rose from 95 to 167. The population of the parish fell from 8,022 in 1841 to 5,873 in 1851,[149] a loss of 27 per cent from a poor parish. Whilst Forkhill retained a significant number of cabins, here also it was mostly the small tenant farmers, cottiers and labourers who, like their unrooted cabins, were missing from the later census. However, the increase in first- and second-class housing in both parishes would suggest an increase in prosperity for those who survived and remained. Thus it was those on the insecure margins of the agricultural system who suffered most.

Writing about the prosperous 'calcareous plains'[150] of the Cooley Peninsula, T. Jones Hughes noted the highest declines in population from the famine era, 1841–61, were in the cottier townlands. Whitestown lost 66 per cent and Rathcor 56 per cent. For Jones, the 'fate of the cottier ... was in marked contrast to the strength and stability displayed by the farmers in the same townlands.'[151] In 1851, the barley fields of Cooley had 'some of the highest land values (over £1 per acre) recorded in Ireland at this time',[152] and the fate of the cottiers had little impact on the economy. Regarding the rundale communities on the poor soil and marginal land in Glenmore above Omeath, Jones noted that between 1841 and 1861 the population of Glenmore declined from 506 to 258 (51 per cent) and Castletown from 805 to 345 (43 per cent).[153]

This evidence at townland and parish level would suggest that regardless of the initial prosperity of the townland or parish it was the small tenant farmers, cottiers and labourers who suffered. Both they and their houses were severely reduced in the 1851 and 1861 censuses. Jones demonstrated that the richer arable townlands of Cooley suffered population loss between 1841 and 1861 simliar to the losses endured on the poorer townlands above Omeath. Between 1841 and 1851, the richer parish of Donaghmore in County Down lost 22 per cent of its population. The poorer parish of Forkhill lost 27 per cent of its population. Both figures are above the average for their respective counties and for Ulster (17 per cent).[154] It was a social famine but perhaps its differential impact is best observed at a micro level.

Giving evidence to the Select Committee on Outrages (Ireland) on 18 May 1852, the Revd Gunn Brown, who had previously given evidence to the Devon Commission, claimed that there were between 600 and 700 Presbyterian families in four congregations around Newtownhamilton, including some in County Monaghan, but 'within the last 20 years above 300 Presbyterian families have disappeared by emigration and the state of the times.'[155] This testimony, alongside evidence from the Harshaw diaries, Quaker evidence from Tartaraghan, near Loughall, and census information from Altnaveigh townland, near Newry, tell of the Famine directly affecting Protestants. Letters to Dublin Castle from other parts of Ulster, from ministers like the Balinderry curate John J. Jackson, tell a similar story. In his parish of 3,362 inhabitants, many of them cottier weavers, 1,022 were destitute.

Those 'parishioners living in 4 townlands of the latter (Co. Tyrone) have never received one day's employment from any Public Works, and they are consequently reduced to the extreme of want – we can only allow them a small portion of meal … & last week a man and his wife died'.[156] The neighbours claimed they died from starvation. Such evidence suggests it was not an ethnic famine.

In South Armagh, one consequence of the famine was a growth in ejectments and related agarian outrages. Giving evidence to the Select Committee on Outrages, the Revd Gunn Brown stated that outrages 'had increased since the failure of the potato crop, when small farmers found it difficult to make up rents ... and landlords and agents commenced evicting and serving notices to quit'.[157] The number of ejectments had increased and if the Revd Gunn Brown had called landlords 'exterminators' 'it would not be contary to the fact'.[158] However, both he and the Revd Lennon, who had also given evidence to the Devon Commission, agreed that there were fair landlords who had and were reducing rents, even if some had delayed in doing so. The Revd Lennon referred to small tenants whose 'circumstances have been very much reduced during the last five or six years, owing to the failure of the potato crop, and the rents not being reduced in time; but I know that they are now contented'.[159] However, many tenants were not content and the conflict between landlord, agent and tenant continued. Between 1841 and 1852, there were seven agararian murders and three attempted murder victims around Crossmaglen.[160] One of the three attempted murders was that of the landlord Meredith Chambre, on 20 January 1852. Chambre lived outside Meigh at Hawtorn Hill on the slopes of Slieve Gullion. A month earler he had received a threatening letter giving the reasons why they would try to kill him:

> Beware of General Avenger, I am not a fool, I am giving you timely warning. Its like the thief of the gallows and you landlords, in the seed of time, if they don't give their tenants seed oats to put in their land and lower the rents, it will be measured in their corpse. And here is Mr Chambre, a beggarman, he had better keep close for if he does not, he may have his coffin ready. We will bury him when he will have neither coffin or shroud around him … I am General Avenger.[161]

Conclusion

Ulster was different. There was a tradition of Tenant Right; weaving was a widespread cottage-based industry and Belfast's mechanised linen industry was expanding rapidly. But one feature Ulster shared with the rest of Ireland was an underclass, identified by the Devon Commission, of small tenant farmers, cottiers and labourers. It was they who depended upon the potato, and when the blight arrived it was they who suffered most. Statistically significant macro distinctions can be made beween the provinces, between the west, the south-west and the rest, but it can no longer be claimed that the Great Famine did not happen in the north; that it did not impact severely upon both communities in the north. Perhaps a full assessment of that impact awaits further work at townland and parish levels, where there were significant differences, even over a few miles.

Around Newry it was a shorter famine, and the numbers emigrating were significant but smaller than through other ports. Newry's ships were not 'sailing coffins' but for a time, especially in 1847, the misery and reported destitution was comparable to that in the west and south-west. The impact of the Famine was differential and micro studies tell of differences between baronies, like Upper Iveagh (Down) and Upper Orier (South Armagh), between townlands and between parishes, like those around Newry. The suffering John Mitchel described on his way to Galway was, for a while, matched in and around his hometown.

On 27 February 1850, a cloudy day with some rain, in the townland of Loughorne, James Harshaw planted 'lumpers on boath sides of the marsh hadge'.[162] Two of his sons were now in America and eight houses that had been inhabited in 1841 had melted into the landscape or were deserted. The population of his relatively prosperous townland had fallen by 62 (or 30 per cent).[163] One of of the dead was his sister, who had caught the fever helping the sick.[164] James Harshaw no longer needed to hand out tickets from the relief committee but the Great Famine had touched both him and his relatively prosperous townland in County Down in the north of Ireland.

Notes

1 J. Mitchel, *The Last Conquest of Ireland (Perhaps)* (Glasgow: Cameron & Ferguson, 1861), p. 219.
2 *Nation*, 7 March 1846.
3 Mitchel, *Last Conquest*, p. 148.

4 Ibid. p. 219.
5 Ibid.
6 J.S. Donnelly, 'The Great Famine and its Interpreters Old and New', *History Ireland*, 3, 1 (Autumn 1993).
7 C. Kinealy, 'Beyond Revisionism: Reassessing the Great Irish Famine', *History Ireland*, 4, 3 (Winter 1995).
8 J. Quinn, *John Mitchel* (Dublin: University College Dublin Press, 2008), p. 90.
9 Kinealy, 'Beyond Revisionism'.
10 Donnelly, 'Great Famine'.
11 B. O'Cathair, *John Mitchel* (Dublin: Clodhanna Teoranta, 1978), p. 13.
12 P. Fitzgerald, C. Kinealy and G. Moran (eds), *Irish Hunger and Migration – Myth, Memory and Memorialization* (Quinnipiac, Conn.: Quinnipiac University Press, 2015), p. 43.
13 Ibid. Gerard Mac Atasney's *Famine in Lurgan/Portadown* (Belfast: Beyond the Pale, 1997) provided a detailed account of the Great Famine in a relatively small area.
14 House of Commons, *Her Majesty's Commissioners of Inquiry into the State of the Law and Practice in Respect to the Occupation of Land in Ireland* (Dublin: H.M. Stationery Office, 1845), pp. 424–6 [hereafter 'Devon Commission']: www.dippam.ac.uk/eppi/documents/11941/eppi_pages/281538 (accessed 10 April 2017).
15 T. Jones Hughes, 'Land Holdings and Settlement in the Cooley Peninsula of County Louth', *Irish Geography*, 4, 1 (1955), p. 171.
16 *Belfast Penny Journal*, 19 July 1845.
17 Devon Commission, *Occupation of Land*, p. 35.
18 Public Record Office of Northern Ireland [hereafter, PRONI], Census of Ireland 1841–51.
19 Devon Commission, *Occupation of Land*, p. 50.
20 Ibid. p. 35.
21 J. Mitchel, *Jail Journal, or Five Years in British Prisons* (Glasgow: Cameron & Ferguson, 1876), p. 15.
22 Quoted ibid. p. 15.
23 Royal Commission appointed to inquire into the occupation of land, 1833–1834, Appendices D–H. 1836 (36), p. 338; http://www.dippam.ac.uk/eppi/documents/11051/ (accessed 10 April 2017).
24 Devon Commission, *Occupation of Land*, pp. 422–5.
25 Ibid. pp. 414–15.
26 Ibid. pp. 397–40.
27 Ibid. pp. 408–11.
28 PRONI, 'The Harshaw Diaries, 1841–1867', D4149: https://www.nidirect.gov.uk/publications/introduction-harshaw-papers (accessed 8 May 2017).
29 Ibid. 3 June 1846.
30 Ibid. 2 November 1846.
31 Devon Commission, *Occupation of Land*, pp. 450–2.
32 Ibid. pp. 404–7.
33 Ibid. p. 405.
34 Ibid. pp. 362–70.
35 Ibid.
36 Ibid.
37 Ibid.

38 F.H.A. Aalen, 'Some Historical aspects of Landscape and Rural Life in Omeath Co. Louth', *Irish Geography*, 4, 1 (1955), p. 269.
39 Ibid.
40 Devon Commission, *Occupation of Land*, p. 363.
41 F.H.A. Aalen, K. Whelan and M. Stout, *Atlas of the Irish Rural Landscape* (Cork: Cork University Press, 1997), p. 323.
42 Devon Commission, *Occupation of Land*, pp. 362–70.
43 Jones, 'Land Holding', p. 169.
44 C. Póirtéir, *Famine Echoes* (Dublin: Gill & Macmillan, 1995), p. 234.
45 Devon Commission, *Occupation of Land*, p. 366.
46 Ibid. pp. 350–6.
47 Jones, 'Land Holding', p. 163.
48 Ibid. p. 168.
49 *Newry Commercial Telegraph* [hereafter, *Telegraph*], 23 September 1845.
50 Mitchel, *Jail Journal*, p. 15.
51 *Parliamentary Gazetteer of Ireland 1844–1845*, vol. 7 (Dublin: Fullarton & Co., 1846).
52 *Telegraph*, 17 November 1845.
53 Ibid. 12 November 1845.
54 Ibid. 3 January 1846.
55 National Archive of Ireland [hereafter, NAI], RLFC2/Z488, letter from Magistrate Singleton to Dublin Castle, 9 January 1846.
56 *Telegraph*, 30 May 1846.
57 PRONI, 'The Harshaw Diaries', 3 June 1846.
58 K. Madden, *Forkhill Protestants and Forkhill Catholics, 1787–1858* (Quebec: McGill—Queen's University Press, 2005), p. 126.
59 Ibid. p. 127.
60 *Telegraph*, 14 July 1846.
61 Ibid. 20 August 1846.
62 Ibid. 24 September 1846.
63 Ibid. 8 September 1846.
64 Ibid. 26 November 1846.
65 Ibid. 30 November 1846.
66 PRONI, 'The Harshaw Diaries', 10 November 1846.
67 *Telegraph*, 5 November 1846.
68 Ibid. 24 December 1846.
69 Ibid. 14 January 1847.
70 Ibid. 8 December 1846.
71 Board of Works, 'Extract from the Journal of Lieut. Griffiths, Inspecting Officer, County Armagh', in *Correspondence from January to March 1847, Relating to the Measures Adopted For the Relief of the Distress in Ireland* (London: H.M. Stationery Office, 1847), p. 88: https://ia600208.us.archive.org/11/items/op1246630-1001/op1246630-1001.pdf (accessed 10 April 2017).
72 *Telegraph*, 12 December 1846.
73 PRONI, 'The Harshaw Diaries', 18 December 1846.
74 *Telegraph*, 8 December 1846.
75 Ibid. 20 February 1847.
76 Newry, Mourne and Down District Council (NMDDC), 'A Letter of Life during the Famine', A letter from Samuel Reid to Lady Garvagh, 18 January 1847:

www.newrymournedown.org/a_letter_of_life_during_the_famine (accessed 8 May 2017).

77 *Telegraph*, 12 January 1847.

78 Board of Works, 'Return showing the Daily Average Number of Persons employed on Roads, etc.', in *Correspondence from January to March 1847, Relating to the Measures Adopted for the Relief of the Distress in Ireland* (London: H.M. Stationery Office, 1847), pp. 54–5: https://ia600208.us.archive.org/11/items/op1246630-1001/op1246630-1001.pdf (accessed 10 April 2017).

79 *Telegraph*, 12 January 1847.

80 Ibid.

81 National Archives of Ireland [hereafter, NAI], RLFC3/2/2/35. Letter from Richard Benson to Randolph Routh, 6 March 1847.

82 Póirtéir, *Famine Echoes*, p. 178.

83 *Telegraph*, January 1847.

84 Mitchel to Martin, 23 June 1844. In W. Dillon, *Life of John Mitchel*, vol. 1 (London: Kegan Paul, Trench & Co., 1888), pp. 141–2.

85 Board of Works, 'Extract from Journal of Captain Brereton, Inspecting Officer, County Down', in *Correspondence from January to March 1847, Relating to the Measures Adopted For the Relief of the Distress in Ireland* (London: H.M. Stationery Office, 1847), p. 91: https://ia600208.us.archive.org/11/items/op1246630-1001/op1246630-1001.pdf (accessed 10 April 2017).

86 Ibid. p. 92.

87 Ibid. p. 240.

88 *Telegraph*, 10 November 1846.

89 Board of Works, 'Extract from Journal of Captain Brereton', p. 240.

90 PRONI, 'The Harshaw Diaries', 9 January 1847.

91 Board of Works, 'Extract from Journal of Mr. Griffith, Inspecting Officer, Armagh County', in *Correspondence from January to March 1847, Relating to the Measures Adopted for the Relief of the Distress in Ireland* (London: H.M. Stationery Office, 1847), p. 240: https://ia600208.us.archive.org/11/items/op1246630-1001/op1246630-1001.pdf (accessed 10 April 2017).

92 Madden, *Forkhill*, p. 130.

93 Devon Commission, *Occupation of Land*, p. 197.

94 The Society of Friends, *Transactions of the Central Relief Committee of the Society of Friends during the Famine in Ireland 1846–1847* (Dublin: Hodges & Smith, 1852), p. 191.

95 Ibid.

96 Ibid. p. 192.

97 *Telegraph*, 2 January 1847.

98 Ibid. 6 January 1847.

99 Ibid. 14 January 1847.

100 Board of Works, 'Extract from Journal of Captain Brereton', p. 92.

101 *Telegraph*, 20 February 1847.

102 NAI, RLFC3/2/8 13. Letter from Mr N. Thompson to Dublin Castle, 20 March 1847.

103 *Telegraph*, 11 March 1847.

104 Ibid. 27 March 1847.

105 Figures from 1845–51 compiled by the author from Fever Hospital reports in the *Newry Commercial Telegraph* for the 1997 Newry, Mourne and Down District Council's Great Famine Exhibition.

106 *Telegraph*, 13 March 1847.
107 PRONI, 'The Harshaw Diaries', 5 April 1847.
108 *Telegraph*, 13 April 1847.
109 The Society of Friends, *Transactions*, p. 242.
110 *Telegraph*, 13 April 1848.
111 Ibid. 20 April 1848.
112 Ibid. 2 April 1850.
113 Ibid. 27 November 1847.
114 *Newry Examiner and Louth Advertiser*, 15 July 1848.
115 *Telegraph*, 8 May 1849.
116 Ibid. 17 August 1848.
117 PRONI, 'The Harshaw Diaries', 17 August 1848.
118 Ibid. 17 September 1848.
119 *Telegraph*, 30 March 1848.
120 The ships studied by the writer for the 1997 NMDDC Great Famine Exhibition were: *Sarah Parker*, 150 passengers; *Arethusa*, 22 passengers; *Marchioness of Butte*, 297 passengers; *Brothers*, 297 passengers; *Seraphine*, 232 passengers; *Chas McLoughlin*, 57 passengers; and *Robinson* 99 passengers.
121 I.A. Glazier, *The Famine Immigrants: Lists of Irish Immigrants Arriving at New York, 1841–1851*, vol. 7, part 1 (New York: Clearfield, 1986), p. x.
122 PRONI, 'The Harshaw Diaries', 2 January 1850.
123 British Parliamentary Papers 1847–48, vol. 47, pp. 397–403: www.theshipslist.com/1847/BPP-1847.shtml (accessed 10 April 2017).
124 P. Collombier-Lakeman, 'The Canadian Press and the Great Irish Famine: The Famine as an Irish, Canadian & Imperial, Global Issue', *Mémoire(s), identité(s), marginalité(s) dans le monde occidental contemporain*, 12 (2015): https://mimmoc.revues.org/1787 (accessed 10 April 2017).
125 P. Murphy, *Together in Exile* (Saint John, New Brunswick: P. Murphy, 1990), p. xv.
126 J.F. Cushing, T. Casey and M. Robertson, *A Chronicle of Irish Emigration to Saint John, New Brunswick in 1847* (Saint John, New Brunswick: The New Brunswick Museum, 1979), pp. 67–9: https://dcms.lds.org/delivery/DeliveryManagerServlet?dps_pid=IE1898252 (accessed 10 April 2017).
127 *Telegraph*, 31 May 1849.
128 Ibid. 20 February 1849.
129 Ibid. 23 September 1849.
130 Ibid. 22 February 1849.
131 Ibid. 19 June 1847.
132 Ibid. 24 March 1849.
133 J. Grant, 'The Great Famine and the Poor Law in Ulster: The Rate-in-Aid Issue of 1849,' *Irish Historical Studies*, 27, 105 (May 1990), p. 30.
134 *Telegraph*, 27 February 1849.
135 Ibid. 22 March 1849.
136 Ibid. 15 January 1850.
137 Ibid. 25 August 1849.
138 Ibid. 1 December 149.
139 Ibid. 21 July 1849.
140 Ibid. 18 September 1849.
141 Ibid. 11 September 1849.

142 Ibid. 6 November 1849.
143 Ibid. 12 February 1850.
144 Ibid. 4 April 1850.
145 Ibid. 17 March 1849.
146 Irish and Local Studies Library [hereafter, ILSL], Armagh. Census of Ireland 1851, Lordship of Newry and Barony of Upper Orier, pp. 182 and 58.
147 ILSL, Censuses of Ireland 1841 and 1851, Summary of the Counties.
148 Ibid. General Tables.
149 Ibid.
150 Jones, 'Land Holding', p. 150.
151 Ibid. p. 163.
152 Ibid. p. 150.
153 Ibid. p. 172.
154 C. Kinealy and T. Parkhill (eds), *The Famine in Ulster* (Belfast: Ulster Historical Foundation, 1997), p. 14.
155 House of Commons, *Report from the Select Committee on Outrages (Ireland)* (London: H.M. Stationery Office, 1852), p. 569: www.dippam.ac.uk/eppi/documents/13235/page/339054 (accessed 11 April 2017).
156 NAI, RLFC/2/18/19. Letter from John J. Jackson to Sir Randolf Routh, 13 February 1847.
157 House of Commons, *Select Committee*, p. 565.
158 Ibid. p. 581.
159 Ibid. p. 557.
160 K. McMahon and T. McKeown, 'Agrarian Disturbances around Crossmaglen, 1835–1855', *Seanchas Ardmhacha*, 9, 2 (1979), p. 303.
161 Madden, *Forkhill*, p. 110.
162 PRONI, 'The Harshaw Diaries', 27 February 1850.
163 ILSL, Census of Ireland 1851, Barony of the Lordship of Newry, p. 182.
164 PRONI, 'The Harshaw Diaries', 16 July 1847.

Chapter Five

John Mitchel: Famine, Slavery and Agrarian Politics

James Quinn

Throughout his career as a journalist, condemnation of the Famine in Ireland and defence of slavery in America were two of the causes that most agitated John Mitchel. He saw no contradiction in condemning one and defending the other, arguing that the Famine had been caused by the heartless and destructive laws of liberal political economy, while an agrarian system based on slave labour was a solid barrier against the ravages of capitalism rather than a system of oppression. He saw capitalism in all its guises as primarily an English system that aimed at a form of conquest and domination more insidious and deadly than that achieved in the past by armed force. Its export he characterised as a peculiarly nineteenth century means of conquest, proceeding across the world by stealth, under the guise of banners such as 'free trade' and 'industrial development'. In reaction, Mitchel rejected all the modernising tendencies of the nineteenth century, seeing them as battering rams used by the British Empire to spread its power and influence across the globe.[1]

In opposing English dominion in Ireland, Mitchel believed he was keeping faith with all those who, from the twelfth-century Norman invasion onwards, had refused to accept the rule of an alien power. He saw himself as working in a long tradition of resistance but, although much given to invoking the ideals of the United Irishmen of the 1790s, his form of nationalism was in fact very different. United Irish nationalism, sparked by the revolutions in America and France, was very much a product of the Enlightenment, inspired by rationalist and progressive principles and aiming at the ideal of a universal future of liberty and fraternity for humankind. Mitchel's nationalism was of a much more Romantic variety: it stressed the power of instinct rather than reason, the destructive potential of human nature rather than its capacity for progress, and the historical differences between nations rather than their common aspirations.

Mitchel was, in fact, quite dismissive of the notion that there had been any such thing as an eighteenth-century Enlightenment at all, finding absurd the notion that Europe was stumbling along in blind ignorance and superstition until the writings of rational philosophers had illuminated the world and shown the way to the promised land of tolerance and benevolence. He believed that it was simply rank arrogance for any era to think itself more enlightened than its predecessor, and that notions of moral or social progress were illusory. In opposition to British Whig historians who traced the onward march of human progress and perfectibility, Mitchel took a cyclical view of history, maintaining that the powerful would inevitably one day be brought to earth, and that their place would be taken by nations which were now weak or oppressed.[2] Confronted by an abolitionist with that classic distillation of Enlightenment thought, the opening lines of the American Declaration of Independence, Mitchel retorted: 'I am not aware that every human being, or any one, has "an inalienable right to life, liberty, and happiness". People often forfeit life and liberty, and as to "happiness" I do not even know what it is'.[3]

For Mitchel, this so-called Enlightenment, with its insistence that the liberty of the individual contributed to the common good, formed the basis of the system of laissez-faire political economy that had destroyed the sense of mutual obligation between landowner and tenant and master and artisan that had held together European society for centuries. He maintained that it promoted a world view in which profit was everything, and factory workers and tenant farmers nothing more than economic units. There was no greater example of the iniquity of this 'enlightened' capitalism than Ireland where, unfettered by any sense of duty or national solidarity, political economy had set in motion an artificial famine. Mitchel argued that the Great Famine was not a natural disaster; instead, the failure of the potato crop had been exploited to clear the Irish peasantry off the land. How could it be said that a country was suffering from famine when in fact it was well-stocked with food and continued to export tons of wheat, oats, beef and butter? People were starving because the British government wanted them to starve. To feed Britain's ever expanding industrial population, Ireland was to be converted into a vast cattle and grain farm. Its 'surplus population', farming their uneconomic smallholdings, was simply an obstacle in the way of British 'progress'. But hunger would soon uproot them from the land, and send them to the poorhouse, the coffin ship or the grave. Ireland, once shorn of its fractious peasantry, would be easier to govern and reconciled to its role within the United Kingdom. England would gain in every way.[4]

This, Mitchel suggested, was all the more effective because it was done under the mask of social improvement. He claimed that the British government was greatly shaken by the vast Repeal meetings orchestrated by Daniel O'Connell in 1843, and realised that revolution in Ireland was prevented only by O'Connell's rigid adherence to a policy of moral force. But O'Connell was ageing, and might one day be replaced by a leader more prepared to unleash the power at his disposal. The government decided therefore that the Empire should no longer be threatened by this dangerous enemy within. Instead they 'were to be thinned, to be cleared off: but all in the way of "amelioration". They were to be ameliorated out of their lives'.[5] This, he claimed, worked so effectively that after a few years the once vigorous agitation for Repeal of the Act of Union had collapsed amidst hunger, evictions and mass emigration.[6]

According to Mitchel, because this happened with such speed and under the cover of famine, most Irish were bewildered and blind to Britain's true intentions. There were, though, a minority of Irish nationalists who, unlike O'Connell, had always distrusted British governments, whether Tory or Whig, and were determined to resist. He described how 'a kind of sacred wrath took possession of a few Irishmen at this period. They could endure the horrible scene no longer, and resolved to cross the path of the British car of conquest, though it should crush them to atoms'.[7] Driven by this 'sacred wrath', Mitchel in his influential *The Last Conquest of Ireland (Perhaps)* portrayed the Famine as the most recent (and most deadly) attempt by Britain's rulers to crush Ireland's demand for self-government once and for all.[8]

This, Mitchel claimed, was a policy with historical precedents: he equated the actions of Lord Clarendon, Lord Lieutenant of Ireland during the Famine, with those of Mountjoy, Lord Deputy of Ireland at the beginning of the seventeenth century, who defeated Hugh O'Neill by means of a ruthless scorched earth policy. But whereas Mountjoy had used fire and sword to devastate the country, Clarendon had inflicted even greater devastation by means of commissions and legislation.[9] The story of the Famine was that of 'an ancient nation stricken down by a war more ruthless and sanguinary than any Seven Years War or Thirty Years War that Europe ever saw'.[10]

In an elaborate conspiracy theory, Mitchel claimed that the true function of the Devon Commission, set up by the government in 1843 to investigate the Irish land system, was to undermine tenants' existing rights to security of tenure and draw up a blueprint for sweeping land clearances. The Commission's report became 'the Bible of British legislators and landlords; the death warrant of one million and a half of human beings, and the sentence of pauper banishment against full a million and a half more'.[11] Within a year of its publication in February 1845, the failure of the potato crop provided an opportunity for its implementation, and the government's manipulation of workhouses and relief schemes helped complete the effects of hunger and disease in demoralising, uprooting and exterminating Irish smallholders.[12]

The claim that the Famine was deliberate genocide was not unique to Mitchel. Even the moderate Charles Gavan Duffy described it as 'a fearful murder committed on the mass of the people'.[13] But it was Mitchel who expressed it most forcefully and memorably. He squarely maintained that '[a] million and half of men, women, and children were carefully, prudently, and peacefully *slain* by the English government. They died of hunger in the midst of abundance, which their own hands created'.[14] Popularising this view of the Famine became his most lasting contribution to Irish nationalism, and sank deep into national consciousness at home and abroad, creating a visceral hatred of the government that was responsible.[15]

Mitchel's arguments were often powerful, but they were not always supported by fact. The Devon Commission, for example, did not instigate or plan a programme of mass land clearances. Its report admitted the beneficial effects of tenant-right and recommended granting some additional protection to tenants. It spawned a modest bill that advocated compensating tenants for improvements, but this was eventually overtaken by the dislocation caused by the Famine and never became law. On the question of food exports, Mitchel's claims were also dubious. Irish grain exports had decreased considerably during the Famine years, while imports of food soared, admittedly after some delay. He greatly exaggerated the deliberateness of British policy, which tended to respond to events rather than operate to a preordained plan.

Although at times unfounded or overstated, some of Mitchel's charges did contain an element of truth. Had food exports been stopped after the disastrous harvest of 1846 and before the import of large quantities of foreign grain in 1847, then some of the worst effects of the Famine might have been alleviated. The throwing of all the costs of famine relief onto

Irish taxpayers from mid-1847, and the insistence that a starving peasantry should carry out heavy labour on relief works of little value, were not the actions of a sympathetic or humane government. Many British officials did in fact see the failure of the potato as a heaven-sent opportunity for implementing a programme of social engineering that would catapult Ireland's backward agricultural sector into the modern age of capitalist farming. Such views were held at the highest level by men such as Sir Charles Wood, the Chancellor of the Exchequer, and by a host of lesser officials. Sir Charles Edward Trevelyan, Assistant Secretary of the Treasury and one of the most doctrinaire advocates of laissez-faire economics, maintained that the Famine was 'a direct stroke of an all-wise and all-merciful Providence' and was 'the sharp but effectual remedy by which the cure is likely to be effected'.[16] The complacent and occasionally callous rhetoric of many British administrators and economists, whose humanitarian instincts were overwhelmed by their devotion to political economy, provided some substance to Mitchel's argument. Clearly, people had died of starvation in a country that continued to export food, while the government had often shown itself more eager to defend private property and to pass coercion acts to disarm and intimidate the Irish peasantry than undertake effectual efforts to relieve the Famine.

When relief measures were adopted, Mitchel dismissed them as evidence of British hypocrisy and part of the overall plan to facilitate the demoralisation and extermination of the Irish peasantry, dubbing them 'contrivances for slaughter'.[17] He was deeply concerned with the moral as well as the physical effects of the Famine. As one who extolled the character and culture of his people, he was most anxious that they should not be seen as craven beggars, and claimed that the poor laws were being used to enervate and enslave them. After a model soup kitchen opened at the Royal Barracks in Dublin, where the poor lapped up their food with chained spoons as Castle officials and Dublin society looked on, he winced with humiliation and exclaimed: 'Oh Ireland! Ireland! Has the very soul withered out of us?' Much of Mitchel's rage at the Famine stemmed from a sense of shame that the Irish peasantry had accepted their fate with passivity. Not only Irish lives, but Irish honour was being sacrificed, and he called on those who were left to take action to save themselves 'that we, too, may not be flung into coffinless graves, amid the bitter scorn and contemptuous laughter of mankind'.[18] Looking back some years later, he admitted that in these years he had acted less out of love for Ireland and more out of 'scornful impatience at the thought that I had the misfortune, I and my children, to be born in a country, which suffered itself to be oppressed and humiliated by another'.[19]

At the root of this 'scornful impatience', there was a fear that the Irish had shown themselves to be the cowering wretches of anti-Irish polemics rather than the noble warrior Celts of Young Ireland propaganda. Mitchel's close ally, Thomas Devin Reilly, gave voice to this fear when, frustrated with the passivity of his countrymen at the height of the Famine, he denounced them as 'the most humiliated, the most pitiable, the most helpless, the most despised people with a white skin on the face of God's whole earth'.[20] If so, it could be argued that the Irish (just like the Africans) were fit only to be enslaved by a superior race – in this case their Saxon neighbours.

Such a conclusion would have invalidated the entire Young Ireland mission of attempting to awaken the Irish people to the fact that they were an historic nation who should determine their own future. Mitchel's response was to argue that the degradation of a formerly noble people had been brought about by the dehumanising and destructive forces of modern industrial capitalism. Irish independence was therefore necessary to the survival of the Irish race. Once cut off from England, Ireland could begin to protect itself from the ravages of capitalism, devising a social system more conducive to the Celtic character that would provide a living for all. In the place of factories Mitchel advocated a system of small-scale workshops, regulated like the guilds of the pre-industrial age, which he claimed had created a secure working environment for their members, fixing wage rates and working hours, and establishing mutual rights and duties between master and man. His idealised social system consisted of sturdily independent artisans in the towns and independent yeomen farmers in the countryside, both enjoying the fruits of their own labour:

> I have always looked with a sort of veneration upon an independent farmer cultivating his small demesne – a rural *pater-familias*, who aspires to no lot but labour in his own land, and takes off his hat to no 'superior' under God Almighty. Tenant right, fee-farm, call his tenure what you will, only let him be sure that where he sows, he and his shall eat, reap and be satisfied.[21]

This view could at times lead Mitchel into making (or publishing) statements that had a strong ring of social radicalism about them. The *United Irishman*, a more militant paper founded by Mitchel in 1848 after leaving the *Nation*, proclaimed that since capital was created by the working man, he should therefore be its main beneficiary but humanity had become so corrupted by 'a demonic process, called civilisation' that the principles of natural justice had been reversed: those who toiled to create wealth were labelled 'men of no property' while 'the men who do nothing, who idle the year round – the fools with long bug-a-boo nicknames and gee-gaws, are held to *own* everything'.[22]

In contrast to the injustice of the Irish land system, there was for Mitchel a naturalness about plantation slavery as it was practised in the southern states of America: in fact he was one of those who argued that, compared with being left at the mercy of the destructive forces of the market, slavery was actually good for the slave. Mitchel was unashamedly racist in his reasoning: he argued that Africans were an innately inferior people who lived in a state of barbarism in their homelands and that 'to enslave them is impossible, or to set them free either; they are born and bred slaves'.[23] He claimed that it was right to go to Africa, where most of the population were already 'slaves to ignorant and brutal negroes', and to buy there as many people as possible so that they could be raised 'out of the most miserable and abject of all possible human conditions, to the comparative happiness and dignity of *plantation hands*. This is right, just and humane. The more slaves from Africa, the better *for the slaves*'.[24]

While racism was a common part of nineteenth-century discourse, there was a harshness about Mitchel's racism that set it apart even in his own day. Part of his intention was clearly to provoke and outrage abolitionists. For Mitchel, the progressive, evangelical abolitionist was the exemplar of the hypocrisy of the age. He despised their Calvinist self-righteousness and dismissed them as ingenuous cranks engaged in crackpot crusades. He scorned their belief in the possibility of human improvement and ridiculed their advocacy of reforms such as pacifism, vegetarianism, women's rights, penal reform, and the abolition of capital punishment. Dismissing abolitionists' tightly circumscribed ideas of philanthropy, he claimed that they blatantly advertised their benevolence towards negro slaves, but were indifferent to the sufferings of poor whites in their midst. These were the very people who talked complacently of the designs of providence while millions in Ireland starved, or who, through their heartless gospel of laissez-faire, worked the factory hands of Manchester or New York into early graves. Until the era of the so-called Enlightenment, Mitchel claimed that people had accepted slavery as part of the natural order of things – it was only in the last 100 years or so that simple-minded do-gooders had begun to challenge a system that had never been questioned by Moses or Socrates or Jesus Christ.[25]

Before he settled in America, Mitchel had already been party to controversies over slavery in the Repeal Association in the 1840s. These stemmed from Daniel O'Connell's fervent opposition and his readiness to chide Irish-American Repealers who refused to speak out against slavery. O'Connell condemned the hypocrisy of Americans who boasted of their love of liberty while tolerating the existence of slavery, and consistently tried to use his stature and authority to persuade Irish-Americans to drop their antipathy to abolitionism. He also intimated that he would refuse any funds from America that came from those who were not willing to speak out against slavery.[26] Thomas Davis and his colleagues at the *Nation* thought that this stance was unwise. Their argument was pragmatic rather than principled, maintaining that the priority of the Repeal Association should be to achieve Irish independence and that they should be careful not to alienate any allies. At a Repeal Association meeting in Dublin in 1844, Davis 'notwithstanding the slavery of the negro' declared his support for the United States as 'liberty's bulwark and Ireland's dearest ally'.[27] The *Nation* insisted that slavery should not be allowed to divide the Repeal Association and that 'the southern states must not have their institutions interfered with, whether right or wrong ... We might as well refuse English contributions because of the horrors of mill slavery'.[28]

On joining the *Nation* after Davis's death in 1845, Mitchel took this policy a step further, to such an extent that his colleague Charles Gavan Duffy maintained that in 1846–47 he had to censor several of Mitchel's articles attacking abolitionism.[29] In this as in many other areas, Mitchel had been much influenced by the Scottish philosopher Thomas Carlyle. In his *Occasional Discourse on the Negro Question* (1849, republished in 1853 with the more inflammatory title *Occasional Discourse on the Nigger Question*), Carlyle had argued that black Africans were an inferior race that had been born to be mastered, and that exploiting them for slave labour was in the natural order of things.[30]

When Mitchel arrived in the US in 1853, less than eight years before the start of the civil war, slavery was *the* issue of the day. He was not long in siding with the slave-holding states of the South against the Puritan abolitionists of the North, and declared his support for slavery in the strongest possible terms. Much of Mitchel's admiration for the South stemmed from the fact that he saw it as a haven from the onward march of industrial capitalism that had conquered much of North America and Europe. Praising its leisurely agrarian character, he claimed that the South was largely devoid of the restless, strident materialism of the North. He believed that North and South were two nations with incompatible social systems, drifting wider apart with each passing year, and that the South must finally secede. 'I prefer the South in every sense', he wrote, 'I do really believe its state of society to be more sound, more just, than that of the North'.[31]

Mitchel's ideal social system of independent farmers and artisans untroubled by the demands of the market may have been a dream, but the slave-holding agrarian economy of the South was a reality, and one he found most appealing. In fact, where there were sufficient slaves to perform the necessary work, he argued that the South was 'the most perfect form of social polity now existing anywhere in the world'. Where others saw cruelty and oppression, he saw a society with a dignified and cultured aristocracy and self-reliant freemen, always ready to assert their rights in arms, and regarded the South as the nearest modern-day equivalent to the classical republics of Greece and Rome he admired so much. In no other country, he claimed, was there such a level of social equality between white men: the law was administered in such an even-handed manner that 'the absolute equality of citizen with citizen, and the impossibility of class legislation, gives men in their intercourse with one another, an independent bearing which is totally unknown in England – in England above all other countries for there every man is both a tyrant and a flunkey – tyrant to those beneath him; flunkey to those above'.[32]

To examine the southern way of life, Mitchel undertook a 2,000-mile journey by rail and riverboat through the cotton states. He visited many plantations and claimed that he had not heard a harsh word nor seen a violent action on any of them. He attributed the 'peculiar gentleness of demeanour and quiet courtesy' of the South to slavery, which he believed had a restraining influence on the slave owner because of the great power and responsibility he carried. The southern custom of speaking gently to servants, 'and so much of the intercourse of the people is with their servants', created throughout society 'a softness of manner and tone which, in educated people, being united with dignity, and self-possession, gives me the ideal of a well bred person'. However, he was well aware that behind all this patrician gentility there was often a violent reality, admitting that there were instances when 'severe measures are sometimes needful in subduing a young negro. What then? Is a colt not to be broken because he is vicious?'[33]

Even in the South, Mitchel was at the extreme end of pro-slavery sentiment. In October 1857, he helped found a newspaper, the *Southern*

Citizen, in Knoxville, Tennessee, to defend the doctrine of states' rights, promote 'the value and virtue of slavery, both for negroes and white men', argue for a reopening of the African slave trade and encourage the spread of slavery into the new territories of the US.[34] Since the reopening of the African slave trade was likely to perpetuate slavery indefinitely, it was supported only by the institution's more uncompromising advocates, and Mitchel's views were not always welcomed by southerners, many of whom thought them excessive and playing into the hands of the abolitionists. One southern paper rebuked him as a self-publicist and 'impertinent foreign meddler' who 'now vapours and struts as if the whole South belonged to him'.[35]

If Mitchel did not perhaps believe that the South belonged to him, he strongly believed that he belonged in the South. While working for the South, he admitted that 'he was thinking of Ireland, and contending for the South as the Ireland of this continent'. [36]

> The opposing interests of North and South were substantially the same as the opposing interests of England and Ireland. The one is the commercial, manufacturing, and money-broking power – the other represents mainly agriculture. England has striven long and hard to make the industry of Ireland subservient to herself … So the Northern States have been labouring to reduce the Southern States from states to provinces … there is even a great and increasing *absentee drain* from the South to the North. Northern 'literature', being cheap and vile, is forced into all our houses; and men of enterprise and of genius at the South go to the North for their career and their reward. You perceive that I am narrating, in part, the history of Ireland.
>
> Moreover I recognise a corresponding difference in the national character of the two sections. The North is more English – The South more Irish. French, Welsh, Spanish – in any case Celtic … The Celtic is the superior breed; of finer origin, more fiery brain, more passionate heart – less greedy, grabbing, griping and grovelling …
>
> In race being Celtic; in pursuits agricultural; in temperament pleasure loving, hospitable and indolent; in position defensive against the commercial spirit of the age – the South is a new Ireland; her rival another England. Can you wonder that I am a Southerner?[37]

But he admitted that while there is 'a sort of parallel between the condition of the southern states and that of Ireland', there were also significant differences: southerners held arms, and did not have a powerful foreign garrison in their midst. 'In short they are strong, free, proud and masters of the situation. The remedy here, as in Ireland, is Repeal of the union. Singular, that your correspondent, in whatever hemisphere he may be, finds himself labouring at repealing of unions. There is nothing like consistency'.[38] This was Mitchel's standard answer to those who accused him of inconsistency in advocating freedom for Ireland and slavery for negroes: 'The liberty which I sought for Ireland was national independence only; and that only was what I sought for the South'.[39]

The different situations in Ireland and the southern states of America, however, called forth very different responses from Mitchel. Because he saw Ireland as the victim of a callously modernising political and social system that had produced starvation and misery for millions, he appears at his most revolutionary in his violent denunciations of British policy in Ireland. His opposition to landlordism and unrestrained capitalism led some later left-wing republicans (notably James Connolly) to praise him as a pioneering social radical.[40] In fact, Mitchel was generally hostile to socialist and communist ideologies, dismissing them as either forms of centralised tyranny or Utopian make-believe.[41] The Mitchel who defended the plantation slavery of the American south is clearly no social radical, but a figure who prided himself on his staunch conservatism, denouncing the irresponsible demagoguery of abolitionists and dismissing the introduction of a democratic franchise in the new territories of the US 'as the pernicious doctrine of squatter sovereignty'.[42]

During the American Civil War, Mitchel travelled from Paris to Richmond, Virginia to assist the Confederacy. (His three sons fought for the South; two of them were killed in action, and one seriously wounded.) Mitchel himself wrote for several southern newspapers, vigorously defending the conduct of the Confederate States and resisting all attempts to interfere with the institution of slavery. When, towards the end of the Civil War, the Confederate government proposed to emancipate slaves who agreed to fight for the South, Mitchel was staunchly opposed, arguing that if freedom was a good thing for slaves, then the South had been in the wrong from the start.[43]

As one of the greatest polemicists in Irish history, Mitchel liked to cast things in stark terms, to assert that modernity and capitalism gave people no real choice between being enslaved by the impersonal forces of the market or enslaving their fellow human beings in the plantations of Alabama. For Mitchel, the Irish peasant and the African slave were sharp opposites, the first with no defence against the cruelty of capitalism, the second fortunate to be shielded from its harshness by the benevolence of his owner. What Mitchel did not concede was that there was common ground between them. Neither was master of his own destiny: the peasant could be uprooted from his home by economic pressure or the decree of his landlord, the slave at the whim of his master. Both made considerable profits for Irish landlords and American slave-owners, who for all their responsibilities and obligations, lived lives of far greater comfort than peasant or slave, and in their outlook, lifestyle and sense of entitlement had much more in common than Mitchel would be prepared to admit. Both the mid-nineteenth-century system of Irish landholding and the plantation slavery of antebellum America were systems of agrarian exploitation that benefited the few at the expense of the many. Opponents may have viewed them as anachronisms with no place in an increasingly democratic world, but both were firmly enough entrenched to require powerful external forces to bring about their demise: in the case of Ireland, a series of radical reforming land acts that transferred ownership of the land from landlord to peasantry, and in the case of America, a bloody and destructive civil war.

But for Mitchel to concede that the Irish peasant and the American slave were both the victims of oppressive and outdated systems would have meant embracing a broader view of the world and admitting that those who sought justice for all, regardless of their nationality or skin colour, were not all misguided Utopians or hypocrites. The tragedy of John Mitchel's career is that this was one reality that he was never prepared to confront.

Notes

1 For Mitchel's opposition to modernity, see J. Quinn, 'John Mitchel and the Rejection of the Nineteenth Century', *Éire-Ireland*, 38, 3–4 (2003), pp. 90–108.
2 J. Mitchel, *Jail Journal, or Five Years in British Prisons* (enlarged edn with a preface by Arthur Griffith, Dublin: M.H. Gill, 1913), pp. 20, 29, 128 n.
3 *Citizen*, 11 February 1854, p. 89.
4 J. Mitchel, *The Last Conquest of Ireland (Perhaps)*, ed. Patrick Maume (Dublin: University College Dublin Press, 2005), pp. 120–1, 141–2.
5 Ibid., p. 72.
6 Ibid. p. 142.
7 Ibid. p. 143.
8 Ibid.
9 Ibid. pp. 138–9.
10 Ibid. p. 218.
11 Ibid. p. 71.
12 Ibid. pp. 68–9, 71–2.
13 *Nation*, 29 April 1848.

14 Mitchel, *Last Conquest*, p. 219.
15 See for example, J.S. Donnelly Jr., *The Great Irish Potato Famine* (Stroud: Sutton Publishing Limited, 2002), pp. 18–20.
16 C.E. Trevelyan, *The Irish Crisis* (London: Longman, Brown, Green & Longmans, 1848), p. 201. On providentialism, see especially P. Gray, *Famine, Land and Politics: British Government and Irish Society, 1843–50* (Dublin: Irish Academic Press, 1999), pp. 96–106, 256–83, 322–7.
17 Mitchel, *Last Conquest*, p. 102.
18 *Nation*, 10, 17 April 1847.
19 W. Dillon, 'Letter to Father Kenyon', *c.*November 1857, *Life of John Mitchel in Two Volumes* (London: Kegan Paul, Trench and Company, 1888), vol. 2, pp. 103–6.
20 *Nation*, 24 April 1847.
21 Mitchel, *Jail Journal*, pp. 69–70; *United Irishman*, 18 March 1848.
22 *United Irishman*, 15 April 1848.
23 Dillon, 'Letter to Father Kenyon', vol. 2, p. 106.
24 *Citizen*, 23 September 1854, pp. 600–1 (Mitchel's italics).
25 *Citizen*, 11, 18 February, 7 October, 25 November, 16 December 1854, pp. 87, 104, 632, 749, 797.
26 D.C. Riach, 'Daniel O'Connell and American Anti-Slavery', *Irish Historical Studies*, 20, 77 (March 1976), pp. 3–25.
27 *Freeman's Journal*, 21 May 1844.
28 'The year of work', *Nation*, 13 January 1844; 'America and Ireland', *Nation*, 9 August 1845.
29 C. G. Duffy, *Conversations and Correspondence with Thomas Carlyle* (New York: Charles Scribner's Sons, 1892), p. 117.
30 On Carlyle's influence on Young Ireland, see J.M. Dugger, 'Black Ireland's Race: Thomas Carlyle and the Young Ireland Movement', *Victorian Studies*, 48, 3 (Spring, 2006), pp. 461–85; and O.D. Edwards, '"True Thomas": Carlyle, Young Ireland and the Legacy of Millennialism', in D. Sorensen and R. L. Tarr (eds), *The Carlyles at Home and Abroad* (Aldershot: Ashgate, 2006), pp. 61–76.
31 Letter to Mary Thomson, *c.*December 1857, in Dillon, *Life of Mitchel*, vol. 2, pp. 107–8.
32 'Tour in the cotton states', 6 February 1858 (*Irishman*, 8 March 1862).
33 Ibid.
34 Ibid. 18 December 1869.
35 *Mobile Advertiser*, quoted in D.G. Lester, 'John Mitchel's Wilderness Years in Tennessee', *Éire-Ireland*, 25, 2 (Summer, 1990), p. 12.
36 'Continuation of Jail Journal', *Irish Citizen* (New York), 25 December 1869; see also D.T. Gleeson, 'Parallel Struggles: Irish Republicanism in the American South, 1798-1876', *Eire-Ireland*, 34 (Summer, 1999), p. 110.
37 'Tour in the cotton states', 21 January 1858 (*Irishman*, 25 January 1862).
38 'Tour in the cotton states', 29 January 1858 (*Irishman*, 15 February 1862).
39 *Irishman*, 1 July 1865.
40 J. Connolly, *Labour in Irish History* (Dublin: Maunsel, 1914), p. 148.
41 J. Quinn, *John Mitchel* (Dublin: University College Dublin Press, 2008), pp. 32–3, 81.
42 'Continuation of Jail Journal', *Irish Citizen* (New York), 25 December 1869.
43 Ibid. 9 July 1869.

Chapter Six

What Can Folklore Tell Us about the Great Famine that Other Documents Cannot?

Cathal Póirtéir

In this chapter we will revisit some thoughts about folklore or oral history as a possible source for the study of the Great Irish Famine of the late 1840s and early 1850s, and consider why this resource has been so underused by academic historians writing about the Irish potato famine and the hunger, death and emigration associated with it. In this context, it is worth noting a change in attitudes among many historians towards oral history, in Ireland and beyond, which has brought it 'in from the cold' in Ireland in the last twenty years or so, and the chapter will also give a brief overview of some of the recent thinking and research which has led to this re-evaluation. For the most part, though, examples will be presented from the oral tradition about the Famine which will allow the reader to form their own opinions as to their value in explaining what happened and how people felt about it.

There are, of course, questions about the reliability of folklore and folk memory of which we should be aware. The information drawn from oral tradition is poor at supplying context or chronology, accurate numbers or analysis. For those we must turn to more traditional written historical sources where these data are easily available. Memories may be selective or distorted, making oral tradition 'an unsafe historian', as John O'Donovan, the nineteenth-century Irish scholar, styled it, but perhaps not uniquely so given the inherent bias or selective and self-serving nature of some diaries and memoirs from administrative, political or religious sources written with an eye to a contemporary audience or future historical assessment.

As far back as 1943, Robert Dudley Edwards supported 'a scientific collection of the oral evidence of the people to be carried out by trained historians under the ICHS [Irish Committee of Historical Science], regarding the history of the last 100 years'.[1] He hoped this oral evidence could be used, in conjunction with contemporary documents, to 'fill in the gaps in the documentary material or in supporting that material'.[2] Indeed, the questionnaire about the Great Famine prepared by historian T.P. O'Neill and issued by the Irish Folklore Commission (IFC) in 1945[3] may well be a result of Edwards' 1943 proposal.

In 1978, Robert Dudley Edwards returned to the subject of folklore and history: 'Methodological developments have made historians more scientific but they may not always have realized how drastically they could be divorced from valuable sources by stressing to rigidity their exclusive reliance on contemporary documentation or on archives, or on professional opinion, influencing them to distrust, if not reject, folk material as literary effusions'.[4] In recent years, University College Dublin (UCD) historian Mary Daly has helped explain the long neglect of folklore as a source for Famine studies: 'The use of folklore for historical inquiry requires a methodological training and a sophisticated understanding of the material that evolved many decades after the founding of Irish Historical Studies, and it is only in recent decades that historians have begun to actively engage with historical memory as a research topic'.[5]

So what qualities does material from the oral tradition offer those interested in portraying the events and results of the Great Irish Famine that may not be easily found in many official documents? The economic historian Cormac Ó Gráda has included research into the folklore of the Famine within his already broad interdisciplinary approach. In *An Drochshaol, Béaloideas agus Amhráin*[6] he evaluates the advantages and disadvantages of folklore as a source and notes that it often contains otherwise unreported or unrecorded personal thoughts about the disaster: 'Choinnigh an dream a tháinig slán – más féidir a leithéid a rá futhu – chucu féin formhór den turraing, den bpéin, nó den náire a bhí gairid don gcnámh. Ar chaoi ar bith, ar éigean má breacadh síos i nuachtán nó má admhaíodh riamh é le lucht an údaráis'.[7] Ó Gráda looks particularly at the songs and poetry which were composed and sung within the Irish-speaking communities which suffered during those years of hunger. He looks for evidence of semi-public feelings about the Famine and connected themes, as exchanged and represented within that linguistic community in song and in poetry. He is not alone in his interest in songs as a source for popular sentiment, and some historians accept that 'studies in public opinion necessitate the evaluation of the ballad'.[8]

In his book, Ó Gráda surveys the use of folklore by historians in societies as far apart as Nyasaland and Alaska, where written sources are scarce or limited in what they record. He mentions particularly the work of Jan Vansina, which emphasised the oral tradition as a corrective to written histories, composed from a colonial perspective or from colonial sources. Vansina emphasises the importance of the view from within a community offered by folklore with the local detail and colour it can supply. Gwyn Prins, another historian quoted by Ó Gráda, advised:

> The historian must also reveal what it was like to have been there … it is to these vital parts of the historian's task that oral history – tradition and reminiscence, past and present – with its detail, its humanity, frequently its emotion and always its scepticism about the entire historiographic undertaking – is best addressed. Without access to such resources, historians in modern, mass-literate, industrial societies, that is, most professional historians, will languish in a pool of understanding circumscribed by their own culture.[9]

In this chapter, and in two compendiums of famine folklore, *Famine Echoes*[10] and *Glórtha ón Gorta*,[11] I draw on the main manuscript collection assembled by the IFC from the mid-1930s. In 1936, the founder and Director of the Folklore Commission, Séamus Ó Duilearga, drew attention to this 'vast amount of material not available elsewhere'[12] and highlighted this untapped resource as a way of explaining and supplementing other sources.

Recent folklore studies demonstrate that local events can be accurately remembered over generations, particularly in traditional societies where the oral tradition remained strong and where the events described were rooted in the local landscape. For example, going back a full fifty years before the Great Famine, in her essay on the dynamics of oral tradition published in *Béaloideas*,[13] Maureen Murphy examined the evidence of the oral tradition against the contemporary written sources and demonstrated that the local events of the 1798 Rebellion were accurately recalled and passed on in the oral tradition of County Mayo, almost 150 years after the events described.

In traditional societies, storytelling and recollections of local events were part of the fabric of a community's understanding of its own history. The local and social contexts helped provide a cultural continuity that conserved local events and details that remained both known and subject to correction if they departed from the traditional telling in any meaningful way.

Nevertheless, given the ravages of time and changing circumstances, we should be aware that as traditional communities and the strength of their oral traditions change, the less likely are the details of narratives to be well anchored in distant historical events. The further removed we are from the events, the more likely the process of oral transmission is to become weaker and less reliable. At another level, community access to a wide range of traditional narrative types may also transform perceptions of an historical event into a common narrative genre, such as the legend. Later, I will refer to some legends which show how a community that valued and taught generosity in adversity through narratives was situated during the Famine.

Roger McHugh offered opinions on the possible disadvantages of the oral tradition as a source for historians as the time between the collection of the material from the events grows: 'with the passage of time, oral traditions tend to become blurred and [their] flavor of personality and of place become weaker'.[14] He also draws attention to the possible advantages folklore might depend on over printed sources. It may 'render more vivid and graphic the picture of the famine as experienced by its sufferers ... adding something human and vivid to our understanding of the past'.[15]

Dealing with 1798, the Israeli scholar Guy Beiner[16] noted the emergence of oral history as a distinct academic field 'taking root all over the world and receiving recognition amongst the humanities and the social sciences, although some prominent historians remain obstinate in expressing their disapproval'.[17] Beiner has also spoken about 'alternative vernacular histories' and 'communities of memory', which provide possibilities for interpretation, and calls attention to the unique characteristics of oral material and its ability to focus on mentalities. Beiner's interest is in 'not only the history of what happened, but the history of what it meant': 'meaning as revealed by narrative and linguistic form rather than fact is what makes oral history different, and a necessary tool for the history of subjectivity'.[18]

Oral history can allow disempowered communities to speak for themselves and about themselves, making a wider range of experiences available to us. Often oral history and folklore can provide us with voices which are otherwise forgotten, marginalised or suppressed. These folk memories may also be personal and subjective, presenting an individual viewpoint of events to an audience. This causes a problem for many historians who prefer objective and contemporary documentary evidence. So we can see that there are advantages and disadvantages associated with the folk material – there are things that folklore is not good at, and others it is good at – when compared with material that comes from a range of other sources.

What the folklore record certainly shows is what the people questioned by collectors thought about what had happened. This is often expressed in a range of locally based narratives, memories and traditions, sometimes prompted by local landscape and archaeology, where memory may be prompted by the spatial and physical: by famine graves, buildings used to distribute relief, the ruins of abandoned houses, roads and walls built as relief works and other changes from Famine times, still visible in the landscape.

It should be remembered that we are talking about communities in which many of the people recorded were occupying the same land for generations since, and perhaps before, the Famine. Many were the descendants of those who remained alive and stayed in Ireland after the Famine, while others are the descendants of families where relations died or emigrated because of the Famine. In Maureen Murphy's work on the oral tradition and the events of 1798 in Mayo, she writes that: 'Where every field is named and, in most places, the names have geographical associations, it is not surprising that, at that time, there was a close relationship between oral tradition and landscape. On the other hand, where place did not play a definitive part in the narrative, the story is likely to be located anywhere or omitted altogether'.[19]

Let us concentrate on the possible advantages of the oral tradition over other sources as we try to compose a comprehensive picture of the events. The oral stories tend to be vivid, simple and pitched at a very human level as family or community memories, expressed with personal feelings and emotions. They also give us an example of semi-public opinions and the community mentality regarding the events surrounding the Famine. They include local detail and colour, local places and events, local people and their stories. So here we have access to material that may not be available elsewhere that can help explain and supplement other sources and perhaps act as a corrective to narratives and perspectives from outside those communities. This approach has sometimes been characterised as 'history from below' or a view from within. It can offer previously unexplored possibilities of interpretation and otherwise unrecorded facts.

So let's explore some examples and see what they have to offer. The following account was collected from Máire Ní Ghearbháin, born in 1874, a farmer's wife from Sraith an tSeagail (Srahataggle), Gleann na Muaighe, County Mayo:

> Mhothaigh mé fhéin sean Tomás Ó Gearbháin ag rá go dtigeadh daoine as áiteachaí eile an bealach seo ag iarraidh bídh. Dúirt sé gur tháinig bean amháin agus go raibh páiste beag léithe. Ní raibh sí i bhfad ins an áit ná go bhfuair sí bás, Dúirt sé nach raibh sé ag déanamh aon smid bhréige go bhfaca sé an páiste a diúl brollach na máthara agus í fuar marbh. Nár chráití an radharc é sin. Dúirt sé go mba é an radharc ab'uafásaí a chonaic sé fhéin riamh é.[20]
>
> I myself heard old Tomás Ó Gearbháin say that people would come this way from other places looking for food. He said that one woman came and she had a little child with her. She wasn't in the place until she died. He said he wasn't telling a word of a lie that he saw the child suckling on the mother's breast, and her stone dead. Wasn't that a heartbreaking sight? It said it was the most terrible thing he ever saw.

From Doire na Mainsear, near Anagaire in County Donegal, Máire Nic Giolla Easbuig, born in 1876, gave this account:

> Bhí tithe ins an cheantar seo a bhfuair a raibh iontu uilig bás leis an fhiabhras agus nár cuireadh duine ar bith acu. Bhí an saol chomh holc ins an am seo agus gur chuma le duine ar bith caidé mar a bhí ag an duine eile. Fágadh achan teaghlach iontu féin agus ní raibh aon duine ag teacht isteach ná amach chucu. Thosaigh na teaghlaigh ag fáil bháis agus bhí an chuid eile acu chomh lag agus fhad fríd a chéile nach raibh said ábalta a dhath a dhéanamh daobhtha ach ligean daobhtha go bhfuair an duine deireanach dá raibh sa teach bás. Bhí a raibh sa teach uilig marbh agus na coirp ina luí thall agus abhus fríd an teach. Níor bogadh as sin riamh iad. Bhí cuid mhór de mhadaí ocracha ag gabhail thart, agus deir said, Dia dár sábháil, go raibh madaí ag gabhail isteach ins na tithe seo agus ag ithe na gcorp.'[21]
>
> There were houses in this area where entire households died with the fever and none of them were buried. Things were so bad at the time that no one cared how anyone else was. Each family was left on their own and no one else entered or left the house. Families started to die and the other people were so weak and far gone that they couldn't do anything for them but leave them alone until the last person in the house died. Everyone in the house was dead and the corpses were lying here and

> there through the house. They were never moved from there. There were lots of hungry dogs going around and they say, God save us, that the dogs were going into these houses and eating the bodies.

We can find many similar memories being recalled all over the country in places where hunger, disease and death took their toll. If we move to the eastern side of the province, we have the following account taken down from a postman, Peter Sloane, born in 1912, from Glenloughan, Mourne Parish, County Down:

> I heard my grandmother say that up in Tullyframe (Mourne Parish, County Down) she knew fine people to be seen lying dead along the roads and in the fields. It seems they fell dead out of their standing and the dogs eating at them.
>
> They mustered up, she said, in bunches like, them that felt getting weak. I heard her say that. And then they went away to some place, away out along like, and one done what they could for the other till they died.[22]

From Ballina in County Mayo we have an account of how the people had to be buried at that time:

> Most of the dead were buried in fields or along the roads. The corpse was frequently wrapped with straw ropes and buried in this way without a coffin. Corpses were sometimes carried to the graveyard on donkeys' backs. Tombstones were not erected as it was difficult to find men with the strength to make the graves. Sometimes a large stone or flag was placed at the head or foot of a grave to mark it out.[23]

From north-west Ulster, we have an account from Niall Ó Dubhthaigh of An Bhealtaine, Gort An Choirce, County Donegal. Born in the 1870s, he was an excellent informant, much recorded by the great collector, Seán Ó hEochaidh:

> Chuala mé iomrá go minic go mbíodh cónracha miasóige acu. Is isteach i gceann acu seo a cuirtí an corp, ansin cuirtí maide trasna faoi, agus d'iompróchadh ceathrar fear chun na reilige é. Nuair a thigeadh said fhad leis an reilig, ní raibh le déanamah ach an lúb a bhaint amach den

> tsábhchán agus an corp a ligean síos ins an uaigh chomh socair agus a b'fhéidir. Bheirfaidís an chónair ar ais chun an bhaile leo ansin, nó ní raibh dóigh ar bith eile acu san am le iad a chur.[24]
>
> I often heard mention that they used a pannier coffin with a moveable bottom. The body would be put into one of these, then a stick was put across under it, and four men would carry it to the graveyard. When they would come as far as the graveyard, all they had to do was remove the loop from the catch and let the body into the grave as gently as possible. They would take the coffin back home with them then, for they had no other way to bury them at that time.

Niall also supplied the telling details of how the distribution of relief food in his area saw the development of certain strategies to get the best possible good from it:

> Cha raibh an brot seo ar an chuid a b'fhearr in amanaí. Chomh maith le prácás feola a bheith ann, chuir said min síos ar an choire mhór seo agus bhruitheadh said an t-iomlán fríd a chéile.
>
> Dhéanfaí lán an choire mhóir de sin dhá uair sa tseachtain, i dtoiseach agus i ndeireadh na seachtaine. Bhí fhios ag na daoine na laethe le teacht agus thigeadh said lena gcuid gugán as achan chearn dó thaobh abhus na paróiste anseo ó Mhín Lárach go Feann an Bhuí. Bhí cuid acu eolach go maith agus ní thiocfadh said ar an chéad mhuintir, agus dá dtigeadh féin, d'fhanóchadh said ar gcúl go dtugtaí ar shiúil an chéad scaid den bhrot.
>
> Ba é an chuid ba lú mhaith den bhrot a bhí ar uachtar, agus siocar an mhin a bheith ag dhul air, bhí fhios acu go luífeadh am mhin thíos ar a thóin, agus go bhfuighfeadh said rud maith láidir go deireannach a mbeadh níos mó mine ann nó a bheadh de bhrot agus b'fhearr leo an brachán seo ná an brot féin.
>
> Chuala mé an tseanmhuintir ag trácht air sin go minic.[25]
>
> This broth wasn't the best at times. As well as the meat mixture, they added meal into this big cauldron and they would boil the lot mixed together.
>
> The full of this big cauldron was made twice a week, at the beginning and end of the week. The people knew what days to come and they

> would arrive with their noggins from every corner of the parish from Mín Lárach to Feann an Bhuí. Some of them were in the know and they wouldn't be the first to arrive, they would hang back until the first lot of the broth was gone.
>
> The least good of the broth was on the top, and because the meal was added to it, they knew the meal would lie down at the bottom of it and they would get a good strong portion late on that would have more meal than broth and they preferred this gruel to the broth itself.

Staying with relief food, we'll move on to south Ulster, to Emyvale, County Monaghan. We can see that when the IFC collected their famine folklore, particularly in the 1930s, 1940s and into the 1950s, the informants were careful to make the distinction between soup kitchens, where emergency food aid was distributed, and 'souperism', where relief was linked with proselytism, which did happen in some areas. I think sometimes now when people hear of a soup kitchen they may wrongly presume that it also meant souperism:

> There was a food kitchen in the townland of Bracagh. Both broth and porridge were distributed. The meal was brought from Newry in carts and this took three days to go and three days to come back. It was usually a protestant farmer's house was chosen for the distribution of porridge. A ladleful was given every day except Sunday, when two ladlefulls were given out on the previous Saturday. The people used to line up with the noggins for their share of the food. There is no account of either souperism or proselytism in this district.[26]

There is a family memory of the famine times from a Miss Anderson, born in 1865 and living in Brooks, Forkhill, County Armagh:

> My grandfather, who was Brooks of course, was the first to bring Indian meal into this part of the country. He brought in a full boatload and had it carted up to keep the people from starving.
>
> You'll see a huge boiler outside here in the shed which was used in the famine years for cooking porridge. It was set up in the board room of the church then of course. It was built-in, of course, and they made porridge in the morning, and soup in the evening. I'm afraid I can't say what kind of soup. The porridge was Indian meal of course. It was

> definitely an individual thing. A charity, I suppose. That's definite. It had no connection with any government scheme to relieve hunger or want. My own grandmother superintended it all.[27]

A similar story was taken down from Mr Gwynn, a Protestant gentleman from Ballymoney, Rostrevor, County Down:

> I mind my father and my grandfather collecting off the gentry to provide for the poor people. Only for that the people would have starved. They had no money. There was plenty of other food although the potatoes all went rotten in the fields, but the people had no money to buy it … The food was bought with this collection and was distributed at the old barracks in Rostrevor. Apart from that, the ladies had a fund of their own to provide for the poor.
>
> In those days, the poor had nothing to provide for them. There was no poorhouse and one had to be set up. With the money collected they bought turf. My father and grandfather attended the meeting many times indeed. The turf wasn't given out at once you see. The poor were careless and wouldn't look after it and, if it was all given out at once, they'd have none of it when the time of year came.[28]

Most of the folklore collected in east and south Ulster was written down by the renowned collector Michael J. Murphy of Dromintee. One of his entries is from Susan Murphy, a farmer, born in 1848, from Dromintee, County Armagh, who could well have been one of his close relations:

> They had this big trough or boiler or whatever it was, oh it was way out (about two yards in diameter from her gesture) and he (Willie Jordan) always had a lot of meal, oaten meal, and they paid him for it too (to make porridge at McGuill's Dromintee). And I mind me going up to a rock above our house (Jordan's, Tifferum) where the roses grew and taking them down and cleaning the roots and all for them and cutting up the leaves, and that went into it (the boiler). And many a time they'd just go into a fields of oats and pull the pressaugh and put that in. There was nothing at all.
>
> And at McGuill's they'd come with their wee tin in their turn and get some, and Willie Jordan was over it. And it wasn't every day they'd make it, but maybe every other day, and it would be in the evening.

> That was the time the priddies went bad. Some died with the hunger, but not many.[29]

And from County Antrim we have Joe Mc Conaghy, born 1892, a farmer from Mullarts, Ramoan Parish, Ballycastle. Talking about what his mother had told him about those times, he said:

> She talked of people being in a coma. They would be waking them [at a wake] and they wouldn't be dead at all. She talked of some man from Carry that was burying his wife that time and the man noticed some movement in the coffin and took the lid off, and his wife was there wondering where she was. She said he had nothing but his overcoat to put around her and take her home and she lived for long after that. It was true enough that, and there were others like it.[30]

Those recollections give us numerous examples of empathy for those who suffered and died during the Famine. They give us a perspective at a personal and local level that we can easily understand. Sometimes this may be vivid, emotional and harrowing, but is always a very human understanding of the disaster and how it played out in that locality.

We find that the people remembered by name are local people involved in relief efforts, food distribution or the enforcement of rules surrounding official relief measures. If any were felt to have been unfair or to have had favourites or had profiteered from such work, they are remembered, as are those remembered for kindness. The names of local or national politicians, government ministers or higher civil servants, often so prominent in the administrative accounts of the famine, do not feature in the folk memory.

Legends

Sometimes oral tradition can take an incident, perhaps initially based on reality, and transform it into a narrative that already exists as a migratory legend in tradition. In fact, one of the ways folklorists define the difference between a folktale and a legend, for example, is the legend's characteristic use of local realities to give the appearance of fact to the magical nature of the events.

In the case of the Famine, we have story types that present behaviour to reaffirm exemplary behaviour and consciously held community values in the face of adversity. Here the local personal names, local place names and the belief that the events did occur as related by the storyteller are central to the success of the legend. The legends are essentially educational tools employed to remind the community of laudable values of generosity and open-heartedness. Legends from the folklore of the Irish Famine follow legend types attested to far beyond these shores and well before the nineteenth century. One common legend involves an act of kindness being rewarded by the miraculous appearance of food in abundance. For example, a legend from Mayo collected from Pádraig Ó Conchubhair, born in 1875, of Ard Mór, Belmullet:

> A Paddy Lavelle lived with his wife in Cross. He was called Paddy Major as he must have been working with Major Bingham. They were very poor as they had no money to earn. Next to them lived another very poor couple, and if one of them was without meal the other woman would give her some.
>
> One day the woman next door came to Mrs. Paddy Major and asked for some meal as she had no time to grind some that day. Mrs. Lavelle had not very much to spare either but she gave her some of it and told her, if she could at all, to bring the meal over to her in the evening. The woman told her that she would have some ground by that time and that she would bring her some.
>
> Evening came and she still did not come with the meal so that Mrs. Lavelle said she would scrape the bottom of the chest and try and get as much as would do the husband for the supper. When she went to the chest and opened it she found that it was full to the top and she dropped on her knees and thanked God.
>
> She was like that when the other woman came in with the meal and she too went on her knees when she saw that the chest was full of meal. Mrs. Lavelle told her to bring the meal home again and to come for some anytime she wanted it. That was the time of the Famine and when the neighbours heard about the meal they all flocked around the house and none of them ever went away empty. They came from far and wide to get some of the meal and stirabout and there was always a pot down on that fire.[31]

I first heard a version of another famine legend from a friend in the Ring Gaeltacht in County Waterford twenty or thirty years ago, when I was on a field trip to record some traditional singers from the area. In that telling, the woman was named as Máire Ní Dhroma, the local composer of one of the few songs about the Famine sung right through until the present day and available as a commercial recording,[32] *Na Prátaí Dubha*, by the great Nioclás Tóibín. This legend, in a similar vein to the first one, is another example of how a generous-spirited woman ignores the advice of her parsimonious husband and receives a fitting miraculous reward. It was told by Ned Buckley from Knocknagree, County Cork:

> I often heard that old Mrs. Cremin, the grandmother of Fr. John Cremin, Lissyconnor, Rathmore, was very good and full of charity to the poor and hungry in the Famine days. She used always boil a lot of potatoes for the meals and she never used the ones left over after diner for either pig or cows or poultry but collected the best of them and put them near the fire in order to have a few of them for any hungry poor person who happened to chance to call at the house for some bite to lessen their mad hunger. A few potatoes half-cold and a basin of milk was a great boon to such starving people and often they went away blessing the house and the owners of it.
>
> Many were the poor mother and father who came to her for one single head of cabbage she had growing in the field. It was poor fare but it kept many a family from starving in those days. A head or a couple of head of cabbage boiled with a pinch of salt were divided out among the family and if they had enough of that they'd be thankful.
>
> One day her husband seeing as much cabbage being carried away went into the house to blame her for giving away the cabbage and asked her did she mean to leave themselves with nothing at all. She denied giving away as much of it and said she only gave away a few heads to a few poor women who were starving.
>
> 'Come out now,' said the man of the house, 'and show me what cabbage is left for ourselves.'
>
> She went out fearing the worst and hoping he would not blame her too much for helping God's poor. When they reached the cabbage field, great was her surprise to find there was not a single head missing out of the whole field. There it was – the whole field of cabbage without the loss of a single head but what was used for their own household. She was greatly surprised and fell on her knees to give thanks to God for thus miraculously saving her from her husband's censure and for acknowledging her kindness to the poor.

> Her husband was speechless with surprise as he knew well she had been giving away the cabbage and refusing none of it. He was as impressed by this miracle that he told her to continue on the way she was doing and that he'd never again object to her helping God's poor.[33]

Again, this is a moral tale showing the possible rewards for charitable giving. Sometimes in these legends a stranger enters the house and is welcomed by a share of the scarce household food. The household is rewarded by the sudden or continuous good fortune of miraculously increased food supplies and the stranger disappears, unseen even by those approaching the house.

Another short example of kindness rewarded and apparently being memorialised in a place name appears in an account that came from Tadhg Ó Briain, a farmer born in 1865 from Curr a Cóimeád, Bantry, County Cork:

> Carraig na Cátha. There was a woman living there in the bad times and she had some oats to plant and she gave all the oats to the poor and she had only the chaff left. When the spring came and the boy came in for the oats to plant it and she had only a bag of chaff, and he brought it out and he shook it and it grew fine oats and the place is called Carraig na Cátha since. 'Tis in Inchegeela or in the parish of Kilmurry.[34]

In traditional storytelling and morality, good is rewarded and badness punished and so it is in the exempla which have gathered around the Famine in Ireland. I have also come across legends, such as the butter-stealing witch with her 'come butter come', more usually associated with May Day traditions but in some instances recast as a Famine legend.[35] This is not surprising in a time when food theft by the needy was rife but often undetected. Mostly, in these not so uplifting legends, meanness is punished by the perpetrator falling ill, suffering misfortune in some way, dying in agony or being condemned to wander the countryside as a ghost in testament to their lack of kindness to others in their time of need.

Even individual phrases may be traced by folk etymology back to the Famine, where it is understood as having come as a divine retribution for the misuse or abuse of bounteous food at some time before. In some ways, this attitude is not a million miles from the idea that the Famine was a visitation from God, a providentialist philosophy that influenced attitudes and government policymaking in London. Local farmers in Moat, County Westmeath, supplied the following explanation:

> So plentiful were they (the potatoes) in pre-famine years that it often happened that farmers filled them into sacks, took them into the markets at Moate, Athlone and Ballymahon, offered them for sale but nobody could be found to buy, so that on the return journey the farmers often emptied them into the ditch on the roadside for 'they weren't worth the sacks they were in'.
>
> Afterwards it was said that the Famine was a just retribution from God for the great waste of food. A local saying which may refer to this is 'a wilful waste makes a woeful want.'[36]

I hope you will agree that the thousands of folk memories, recollections, legends and songs about the Great Famine add a depth of understanding about that disaster and its consequences. They have a particular viewpoint that can often cast a light on small human details that might otherwise escape our attention.

I am grateful to those who passed on these traditions, and to those who have collected and archived them.

Notes

1 Memorandum on behalf of the Irish Committee of Historical Science (ICHS), quoted by M.E. Daly in '"The State Papers of a Forgotten and Neglected People"; The National Folklore Collection and the Writing of Irish History', *Béaloideas, The Journal of the Irish Folklore Society*, 78 (2010), p. 68.

2 Daly, 'The State Papers', p. 68.

3 N. Ó Ciosáin, 'Famine Memory and the Popular Representation of Scarcity' in I. MacBride (ed.), *History and Memory in Modern Ireland* (Cambridge: Cambridge University Press, 2001), p. 98.

4 R.D. Edwards, 'An Agenda for Irish History, 1978–2018', *Irish Historical Studies,* 16 (1978–79), pp. 3–19, reprinted in C. Brady, *Interpreting Irish History* (Dublin: Irish Academic Press, 1994), p. 60 and quoted in Daly, 'The State Papers', pp. 69–70.

5 Daly, 'The State Papers', p. 65.

6 C. Ó Gráda, *An Drochshaol, Béaloideas agus Amhráin* (Baile Átha Cliath: Coiscéim, 1995).

7 Ibid. p. i.

8 Edwards, 'An Agenda for Irish History', quoted in Daly, 'The State Papers', pp. 69–70.

9 G. Prins, 'Oral History', in P. Burke (ed.), *New Perspectives on Historical Writing* (Cambridge: Polity Press, 1991), pp. 114–39, quoted in Ó Gráda, An Drochshaol p. ii.

10 C. Póirtéir, *Famine Echoes* (Dublin: Gill & Macmillan, 1995).

11 C. Póirtéir, *Glórtha ón Gorta* (Baile Átha Cliath: Coiscéim, 1995).

12 S. Ó Duilearga, 'An Untapped Source of Irish History', *Studies: An Irish Quarterly Review*, 25, 99 (September 1936), p. 399 quoted in Daly, 'The State Papers', p. 61.

13 M. Murphy, 'Ballinamuck Re-visited: The Dynamics of Oral Tradition', *Béaloideas*, 80 (2012), pp. 38–51.
14 R.J. McHugh, 'The Famine in Oral Tradition', in R.D. Edwards and T.D. Williams (eds), *The Great Famine: Essays in Irish History* (Dublin: Browne and Nolan, 1956), p. 391.
15 Ibid. p. 392.
16 G. Beiner, *Remembering the Year of the French: Irish Folk History and Social Memory* (Madison: University of Wisconsin Press, 2007), p. 18.
17 Beiner, *Remembering*, p. 18.
18 G. Beiner, 'Bodhaire Uí Laoire: Oral History and Contemporary Irish Historiography', Pages (Journal of University College Dublin Arts Faculty), 6 (1999), p. 11; www.ucd.ie/pages/99/articles/beiner.html (accessed 9 May 2017).
19 Murphy, 'Ballinamuck Re-visited', p. 42.
20 Quoted from National Folklore Collection, in Póirtéir, *Glórtha*, p. 135.
21 Ibid. p. 128.
22 Quoted from National Folklore Collection, in Póirteir, *Famine Echoes*, p. 97.
23 Ibid. p. 192.
24 Ibid.
25 Quoted from National Folklore Collection in Póirtéir, *Glórtha*, p. 73.
26 Quoted from National Folklore Collection in Póirtéir, *Famine Echoes*, p. 140.
27 Ibid. p. 146.
28 Ibid. pp. 147–8.
29 Ibid. p. 147.
30 Ibid. pp. 184–5.
31 Ibid. p. 263.
32 M. Ní Dhroma, *Na Prátaí Dubha*. Recorded by Nioclás Tóibín on *Rinn na nGael* [CD] (Dublin: Cló Iar-Chonnachta, 1999): https://www.youtube.com/watch?v=GPTe2GQwRDQ (accessed 9 May 2017).
33 Quoted from National Folklore Collection, in Póirtéir, *Famine Echoes*, pp. 266–7.
34 Ibid. p. 269.
35 Ibid. p. 271.
36 Ibid. p. 38.

Chapter Seven

'Remembrances of Love and Duty': Famine Remittances to Ireland during the 1840s

Ciarán Reilly

> [H]undreds, to my knowledge, have sent home 30 per cent of their earnings in this colony; the numerous letters it has been my painful lot to read, within the last three months, tell a fearful tale of the sufferings of the people at home – parents struggling with want, and children inmates of the poor-house.[1]

> [N]o Irishman would, while he had money, allow his friends around him to starve! One fact was worth a thousand arguments, the poor emigrant girls who had come to this colony within the last two years, had sent home more than 2,000 Pounds to their relatives and he was sure that 3,000 would be sent this way, which was much better than laying it out in milliners shops.[2]

For the million or so emigrants who left Ireland during the hungry 1840s (and immediately after), the memory of their home was never far from their thoughts. In particular, Famine emigrants were anxious that parents and family members would be free from the continued threat of hunger and eviction. When enough money had been saved, they remitted money to family and friends for the purchase of a ticket so that they too could undertake the emigrant voyage. Indeed, during the course of a debate in the House of Commons in 1851, Lord John Russell, British Prime Minister, claimed that more than £1.5 million had been sent to Ireland in emigrant remittances since the Famine had commenced six years previously.[3] While

Russell may have greatly underestimated the actual amount, during the course of the next three decades remittances from emigrants continued to stream into Ireland.

As David Fitzpatrick has argued, over £34 million was remitted to the United Kingdom between 1848 and 1887, most of which went to Ireland.[4] This money, as it trickled into every town and village in the country, provided a means of survival for many and helped fund emigration for thousands of others. Indeed, a survey of Irish newspapers from the late 1840s and early 1850s confirms this, with almost daily reports of people emigrating once they had received remittance money.[5] While the majority of remittances funded individual or family voyages, in certain parishes there was evidence of collective appeals to send remittances so as to induce neighbours and friends to leave. This was particularly true of areas which were devastated by eviction and clearance.[6] Communal remittances by emigrants were often seen as the safest method of transferring money. In April 1847, for example, P.R. O'Reilly, an emigrant in New York, sent remittances for the relief of the poor of Cootehill, County Cavan. Writing to the *Anglo-Celt* newspaper, O'Reilly remarked that most of the money had been gathered amongst Cootehill emigrants and that:

> I have the pleasure to forward the enclosed order for £11, the amount of a subscription entered into by the people of Cootehill and its immediate vicinity, resident in New York and Brooklyn, for the relief of their old neighbours in this season of distress. The sum is small, but there are few of us that have not paid to several collections made here for the most distressed districts of Ireland … I feel doubly proud since we commenced this little collection, for nothing could exceed the gladness with which everyone subscribed.[7]

For most Irish Famine emigrants, remittances were simply 'remembrances of love and duty'[8] which made 'many an aged mother or fathers' heart … to sing with joy' on receipt of the so-called 'American money'.[9] (Of course remittances came from across the globe and not just the United States of America.) This chapter examines the significance of these remittances to Ireland during the Famine years. Taking the business of Abraham Bell, a shipping merchant, as a case study, this chapter provides an insight into the world of the Famine emigrants allowing us a greater understanding of the process of emigration.

In the 1860s, in his history of the Irish in America, John Francis Maguire (1815–72) made particular mention of the importance of remittances which Famine emigrants had sent over the ensuing two decades. Interestingly, Maguire also provided some insight into the character of Irish emigrants, remarking that in smaller cities and towns the remittances were far greater owing to the fact that there were fewer vices or distractions on which emigrants could squander their money.[10] Remittances were crucial in promoting chain-migration and a dependence on the receipt of the 'American money' quickly grew. According to the *Nenagh Guardian* newspaper, every village had four to five orders a week coming from America, thereby facilitating the emigration of others.[11] Indeed, such was the scale of emigrant remittances that many villages were emptied of people. In Lusmagh, King's County (now Offaly), for example, it was claimed that there was not a man in the parish who was not in receipt of money from America.[12] Such was the frequency with which remittances were sent to would-be emigrants that even Charles Bianconi's coaches were said to have been overburdened bringing people to the docks. On one day in March 1853, for example, over 150 people were brought from Clonmel to Waterford port for emigration.[13] Likewise, in Killeshandra, County Cavan, it was claimed that seven coaches, instead of one, passed through the town on a daily basis conveying emigrants to the boat.[14]

The social background of the emigrants mattered little, and even the poorest were able to send some amount of remittance within a few months of their arrival in America, Australia, Canada or elsewhere.[15] Some were substantial amounts. In 1852, a man in County Armagh was reported to have been sent £92 by his daughter.[16] Similarly, on a single day in January 1853, £300 was received at Newmarket on Fergus post office in County Clare. On the same day, at Limerick post office, seventy registered money letters were received from Melbourne, Australia, ranging from £50 to £500.[17] As one contemporary quipped, 'from the great amount that is coming, one would be led to believe that there is a spirit of rivalry in the remittances'.[18] Given the vast sums which were arriving, some commentators ventured to suggest which port had brought the largest remittances.[19] These 'remembrances' to family and friends were also followed by money sent to the priests and bishops, as masses were offered for loved ones who had already succumbed to the ravages of famine.[20] Indeed, priests were often a favoured method of many for sending remittances, as they were deemed trustworthy to deliver money to family members.[21] In 1853, for example, Mary Connors of Kenmare, County Kerry, sent her remittances to the parish priest Fr O'Sullivan, while at Maynooth, County Kildare, the bursar of St Patrick's Pontifical College, the Revd Thomas Farrelly, was a regular recipient of remittances on behalf of parishioners.[22]

The receipt of money was often the first correspondence with the emigrant after their departure, bringing to an end a period of anxiety for the family. Indeed, given the frequency of newspaper reports outlining the loss of emigrant ships such fears were well founded. In the case of the money (£2 8s) remitted to Honora Brosnahan of Scartaglen, County Kerry, in August 1852, for example, there were continued worries about family members who had not been heard of since they arrived in New York.[23] The flow of remittance money to Ireland generally increased towards the end of the summer months, as many were reluctant to leave before farming duties had been completed. With the harvest gathered, the rush for America could once more ensue.[24] By 1853, such was the exodus of labourers from Galway it was reported that with the impending harvest season labour was 'scarce' in the county.[25] Even those employed on relief schemes were anxious to leave. In November 1851, it was reported that out of 200 men engaged on drainage works at Ballinasloe, County Galway, fifty were preparing to emigrate after receiving money from America.[26] The situation was similar elsewhere and 'everyman who can collect £3 is rushing away from the neighbourhood'.[27] Understandably, remittances were not looked on favourably by some, particularly where many of the skilled population were leaving.[28] Servants were also among those who undertook to emigrate, safe in the knowledge that there would be plentiful work for them in America.[29] In one week in April 1853, thirty-five servants emigrated from Dungarvan, County Waterford, following the receipt of remittances.[30] Accompanied by glowing accounts of wages and land, it was difficult to counter such optimism.[31] However, there were frequent warnings that not all emigrants would quickly share in such wealth and those that did had to work extremely hard.[32]

Be that as it may, it seems age was no barrier to emigration and many of those in receipt of remittances were elderly parents.[33] For those who could not undertake emigration, or who did not wish to, the remittance money provided security allowing a family to remain on the land.[34] For others it provided the means to leave the dreaded workhouse. Indeed, towards the end of the Famine a large proportion of inmates in the workhouses waited patiently for money to be remitted to the guardians so that they could leave at once. In August 1851, in Newcastle West in County Limerick, no fewer than seventy men discharged themselves in one week following the arrival of the remittances.[35] It was unsurprising that those who had themselves experienced the horrors of the workhouse were quick to send help to family and friends. Within a year and half of her departure to Australia, Mary Brophy, one of the so-called 'Earl Grey Orphans' who was assisted in emigration from Mountmellick workhouse in Queen's County (Laois) in 1851, sent her mother £4 in remittances.[36] Undoubtedly, the assistance provided by Brophy and her fellow emigrants was a welcome solution for poor law guardians to the problem of overcrowding in Irish workhouses. The captain of an American ship which carried remittances 'by almost every packet that reached Liverpool' commented on the workhouse situation:

> I had occasion, when in Ireland, when visiting a large union workhouse, containing between two thousand and three thousand inmates, to enquire if many such sums found their way to the paupers in that establishment, and I was informed that from six to eight persons weekly on an average were enabled to leave the workhouse by this means, and to pay their passage to America.[37]

The remainder of the money was usually used to buy a suit of clothes, an essential perquisite for prospective emigrants.[38]

The arrival of 'American' money in towns and villages was well publicised, in most cases arriving through the local post office. As remittances were used to pay rent, arrears and shop bills, naturally the arrival of money was carefully watched by landlords, their agents and others. At Ferbane in King's County, for example the landlord, the Revd Henry King, was regularly informed by his land steward, Robert Nugent, that recalcitrant tenants were in receipt of this 'American' money. This information was eventually used to force tenants to pay their rent and arrears to the estate.[39] While it is not possible to ascertain just how many unscrupulous agents like Nugent watched the arrival of the post so carefully, in other instances landlords were happy to act as facilitators of remittances. In Villierstown, County Waterford, for example, the landlord held money in trust for the children of former tenants who had emigrated.[40] Likewise, on the Godfrey estate in County Kerry the landlord played a pivotal role in facilitating the delivery of remittances which were then used to procure medical care amongst other things.[41] Moreover, land agents like Joseph Kincaid, of the Dublin land agency firm of Stewart and Kincaid, delighted with the 'small sums of money being sent over by persons who emigrated in former years' as they assisted other family members 'to go out this Year'.[42]

***

Spearheading much of the remittance drive was the Irish Emigrant Society, which expanded its activities to found the Emigrant Savings Bank in 1850.[43] According to Casey, in the first year of the Emigrant Savings Bank, the Irish Emigrant Society remitted the modern equivalent of $4.6 million to Ireland.[44] The Society published widely these stories of 'emigrant successes' and suggested to the reader that a better life lay before them, and of course the rapidity of raising remittances was evidence of this.[45] However, the Society also played another important role in providing assistance and security for those who were cheated of their savings by 'roguish clerks', who 'imposed on the ignorance of the unspecting poor Irishmen'.[46] By 1851, such behaviour formed the backdrop for calls to form an Emigrants Protection Society, which for many would protect the huge volume of remittances which passed across the Atlantic Ocean.[47] Clearly, businesses and individuals profited from facilitating the return of remittances, in particular banking institutions which were hopeful of improved revenues advertising that all 'letters of credit on New York and Philadelphia' would be 'payable on demand'.[48]

Likewise, the various shipping agents who carried remittances profited from this global flow of money to Ireland. For example, in Cork, it was estimated that three-quarters of all remittances to the county were brought by Morris Hamilton and Company, while in Dublin, James Miley, whose offices were located at Eden Quay, controlled much of the transport of 'money orders' in the east of the country. Despite this there were continued debates about the safety of moving money from America to Ireland.[49] Certainly, great faith was placed in the hands of those who were responsible for carrying this hard-earned money to its destination. Occasionally, the failure of a company meant that emigrants lost out on money which was sent home, which in turn might suggest that the actual figure sent to Ireland was far greater than previously expected.[50] This was certainly true of the demise of Harnden & Company of New York and Liverpool, who by 1850 controlled most of the transatlantic trade. Indeed, throughout Ireland local agents proudly advertised that Harnden controlled 'three fourths of all the remittances … a great fact and proof of unexampled confidence and most honourable dealings'.[51] However, the demise of Harnden in 1851 resulted in the loss of Irish emigrant remittances of almost £12,000, although some was eventually recovered.[52]

***

Another who saw a lucrative trade in emigrant remittances was Abraham Bell (1778–1856), a businessman who was among a number of Ulster emigrants who had settled in New York in the early years of the nineteenth century. A Quaker, Bell quickly built up a shipping firm, Abraham Bell & Company, where he emerged as one of the leading merchants in the city. Operating on a number of transatlantic routes, Bell & Company shipped a wide variety of goods to America and Europe, including linen, glass and candles. With offices in Boston, New York and St Louis, Bell's Irish affairs were handled from 14 Tomb Street, Belfast.[53] By the mid-1840s, his business empire stretched far beyond conveying remittances to Ireland and during this time business boomed. Return ships brought cargo for auction in the main towns and villages in Ulster, where he acted as an agent for Lloyds of London.[54] By 1849, Bell was so successful that he looked to recruit agents in all of the major towns in the north of Ireland, who would provide prospective emigrants and ready markets for goods on the return voyage.[55]

The surviving records of Bell's company are scattered across a number of American university libraries and archives. One collection, located at the New-York Historical Society, provides a remarkable insight into the world of Famine emigrants and their families.[56] Providing details of the recipient, their address and the amount of remittance, the details of these 'bills of exchange' inform on the nature and process of emigration. For the purposes of this study, a sample of over 200 recipients to whom Bell delivered remittances was examined. Hundreds more are unidentified by location, or at least the surviving records of Bell's do not elucidate on their background. In this sample the average return was just over £6. Indeed, contemporary commentators believed that the average sum was about £3, just under the average price of a passage to America.[57] However, many of the individual remittances were much larger; Owen Corcoran, from Ballyhaise, County Cavan, for example, received £11 from St Louis in August 1852; James Gann from Enniskillen, County Fermanagh, received £12 the following month, while the widow Mary McCaffery, also of Enniskillen, received £20. Presumably, such high remittances were intended to fund entire families to emigrate. Those such as James Cox in Newbliss, County Monaghan and

Mary King in Tullyvin, County Cavan, were at the other end of the scale, receiving £3 and £2 respectively, which would help towards the cost of passage, then estimated to be around £3. While admittedly the sample is quite small, the geographical spread also provides interesting information on the spread of Famine remittances.

Of the 200-plus recipients examined in this study, few appear to be located on the western seaboard (stretching from Donegal to Cork), although emigration was often particularly high in these counties. However, this did not mean that Bell's network failed to penetrate the western counties, as examples from Kilmacrenan, Ballyshannon and Castlefin in County Donegal testify. Perhaps the overall geography of recipients reflected Bell's distribution network in the country, with many northern recipients including those located in Strabane, County Tyrone; Forkhill, County Armagh; Glenarriff, County Antrim and Newtown Limavady, County Londonderry. In some instances the name and county of the recipient is all that was given and it would be interesting to ascertain (although probably impossible) whether that money was ever received. For example, how easy was it to identify Mary Flaherty in 'Galway', Mary McNeill in 'Roscommon' or the veritable Michael Murphy of 'Cork, Ireland'? Likewise, the transcription of names frequently posed a problem, not least in the case of 'Ciaran Whelan' of Maryborough (modern day Portlaoise) in Queen's County, which was transcribed phonetically as 'Keyran Whalen'.

However, using contemporary sources, including Griffith's Valuation and estate records, it is possible to identify many of the individual recipients. For example, William Larkin, the holder of twelve acres of land near Ballylinan, Queen's County, survived the Famine and in the 1880s his family was later involved in the major land agitation against their landlord, the Marquis of Lansdowne. Likewise Joseph Anderson, who was in receipt of £4 from St Louis in August 1852, was a merchant in Athy, County Kildare, and during the Famine tendered to the Athy Board of Guardians for turf.[58]

Despite Bell's best efforts in delivering the 'American money' it was common for disputes to arise over drafts. In August 1852, Catherine Cooney of Bruff, County Limerick, for example, claimed that she hadn't received money ($25) which had been sent to her by her son, Daniel Cooney in Philipsville, New Jersey. Writing on his behalf, Curry & Robinson in Marysville, Union County, Ohio, wished to resolve the matter as Cooney, they claimed, 'is an uneasy being and will be in torment until the matter is resolved'.[59] While Bell appears to have been honest and attentive in his dealings, some of his agents may have been questionable in their actions. Some agents were reluctant to part with remittances where the recipient was not intent on emigrating. In many instances their aim was to prevent the Commissioners of Emigration from 'handling it' (the money) as it was often they who wrote seeking the money in the first place.[60]

The success of Bell and others was all the more remarkable given the imprecise nature of the transaction. In the majority of cases no townland was given, so a level of investigation must have taken place as money orders were sent throughout the country. As a result of such lack of information often cited on the bills of exchange, there was little that could be done when money did not arrive at its destination. A poor woman in Blackpool, County Cork, for example, sought the advice of the constabulary when a money order from her daughter in Nashville, Tennessee failed to arrive. Her quest, however, eventually fell on deaf ears.[61] According to a correspondent to the *Cork Examiner,* money was 'apt to go astray' as the 'badness of the writing or the absence of the name of the post town are the things which must puzzle our post offices' thus leading to confusion.[62] The post offices were not entirely blameless in the situation, however, and according to one County Kerry source 'extra' postage was charged by unscrupulous postmasters for 'American letters'.[63]

The Bell 'bills of exchange' also provide other remarkable details about the recipients. For example, in the bills which were remitted from St Louis in 1853, the recipients were overwhelmingly female, suggesting that their male counterparts had gone ahead and were now funding the voyage for other family members. There were also a significant number of widows in receipt of remittance money: the 'Widow' Elizabeth Murphy in Ferns, County Wexford (£2); the 'Widow' Margaret Wallace in Clones, County Monaghan (£3); and the 'Widow' Catherine Walsh of Rathdowney, Queen's County (£5). The remittances suggest the further break-up of the family after the death of a head of the house during the Famine years. As already alluded to, priests were often the recipients of emigrant remittances: in County Tipperary, the Revd Dr Laffan of Fethard and the Revd Thomas O'Connor of Templemore among them. Doctors too were entrusted with delivering remittances, including Dr James Rusk of Bailieborough, County Cavan.

***

Famine remittances played an important role in Irish life during the famine years and in the decades after. Thousands of people depended on the arrival of 'American' money either to fund emigration or simply for survival. As one County Kerry man wrote, the remittance was 'a relief most timely'.[64] Abraham Bell was just one of a number of businessmen who facilitated the transfer of remittances to Ireland during the 1840s and 1850s. While remittances were only part of the process, they do provide a remarkable insight into just how emigration functioned during the Irish Famine. Undoubtedly, without the remittances, emigration would never have reached the levels it did. During 1850 alone, the emigration and shipping firm, Miley, paid £25,000 on 'money orders' from New Orleans, varying from £2 to £20.[65] Likewise, from Australia, Mrs Chisholm organised the remittance of thousands of pounds from emigrants.[66] By 1854, it was claimed that a parish in County Wicklow was receiving almost £1,000 per month in remittances.[67] Such was the vast amount of money which was being sent to Ireland that the British government was urged to establish a money order exchange to oversee the exchanges.[68]

However, in some areas of the country it was lamented that the 'remittance fever' was now slowing down, or at the very least the rate remitted was declining.[69] Nevertheless, these were extraordinary acts of kindness and would live long in the memory of those who received them. As Jacob Harvey, the prominent Irish merchant in New York, reminded people: 'no public meetings were called, no special addresses made to induce the poor Irish to remember their friends at home; their own native charity, and love of kindred, required no such extraneous efforts to bring forth fruit'.[70]

Similarly, further praising the efforts of Irish emigrants in remitting money, the *Cork Examiner* noted that: 'god only knows the amount of generous sacrifice that went to make up this remittance – the stomachs which were pinched for it – the backs which were neglected'.[71] These remarkable acts of giving also extended to neighbours and friends even where it was unlikely that they would ever be reunited. The *Freeman's Journal*, for example, praised the generosity of one poor emigrant woman who continued to send remittances to buy clothes for the children of her former friends.[72]

The remittance of money from Famine emigrants challenges the stereotypical representation of the 'drunken' and profligate Irish who failed to assimilate into American society. While the remittances alone were not enough to stem the tide of hunger and eviction, they certainly were a great help. One can only imagine the further devastation had these remittances not arrived in Ireland during the 1840s and 1850s. The emigrant remittances also explain the unusually large deposits in provincial banks in Ireland during the Famine years.[73] The arrival of this money, particularly the large amounts, also suggests that many of those leaving Ireland were not merely 'famished' emigrants and in many cases left with some degree of prosperity. As Tyler Anbinder has suggested, it is time to 'move beyond the rags to riches story'.[74]

To do so we must follow the journey and experience of the Irish Famine emigrant and their families. Bell's papers provide the opportunity to recover and record the flow of money to towns and villages across Ireland. The records are also of huge importance for family and local historians, and may provide some clues as to Famine genealogies. For example, the Bell remittances may provide the information necessary to ascertain the social backgrounds of the Famine Irish. Were these emigrants from the strong farmer class which the *Belfast Newsletter* reported were leaving from counties Limerick and Tipperary in such numbers (1,200 people) bringing with them sums between £20 and £200? Remittances continued to play a part in Irish life long after the Famine, and contemporary commentators believed that there was no end to this money coming from the veritable 'el dorado'.[75] Indeed, the fact that the Irish Exchequer included emigrant remittances in its National Income Estimations up to the 1960s was further proof of this. These 'missives of unforgetting love and charity' which commenced in earnest during the years of the Great Famine played a crucial role in modern Irish history.[76]

Notes

1 *Morning Chronicle*, 8 April 1846.
2 *Bell's Life in Sydney and Sporting Review*, 5 September 1846.
3 *Cork Examiner*, 8 August 1851.
4 D. Fitzpatrick, *Irish Emigration 1801–1921* (Dublin: Economic and Social History Society of Ireland, 1984), p. 21.
5 See for example, *Freeman's Journal*, 25 October 1853.
6 *Kerry Examiner*, 31 May 1850.
7 *Dublin Evening Post*, 15 May 1847.
8 *Nenagh Guardian*, 13 April 1853.
9 Ibid.
10 J.F. Maguire, *The Irish in America* (New York: Longmans, Green and Company, 1868), p. 322.
11 *Nenagh Guardian*, 13 April 1853.
12 C. Ó Murchadha, *The Great Famine: Ireland's Agony 1845–1852* (London: Bloomsbury Academic, 2011), p. 142.
13 *Kerry Evening Post*, 26 March 1853.
14 *Freeman's Journal*, 19 April 1853.
15 *Leinster Express*, 2 April 1849.
16 *Freeman's Journal*, 13 October 1852.

17 *Belfast Newsletter*, 12 January 1853.
18 *Nenagh Guardian*, 13 April 1853.
19 *Kerry Evening Post*, 27 July 1853.
20 See for example, *Irish Examiner*, 9 June 1854.
21 *Connaught Telegraph*, 12 April 1854.
22 'Bell Papers', New-York Historical Society.
23 See for example, *Boston Pilot*, 21 July 1855.
24 See for example, *Kerry Evening Post*, 15 September 1852.
25 *Freeman's Journal*, 6 May 1853.
26 *Cork Examiner*, 5 December 1851.
27 *Kerry Evening Post*, 6 September 1851.
28 *Freeman's Journal*, 7 April 1853.
29 *Kerry Examiner*, 17 May 1850.
30 *Nenagh Guardian*, 13 April 1853
31 *Cork Examiner*, 10 September 1851.
32 *Kerry Evening Post*, 15 October 1853
33 *Freeman's Journal*, 1 March 1853.
34 *Freeman's Journal*, 12 April 1853.
35 *Kerry Evening Post*, 6 September 1851.
36 *Leinster Express*, 25 December 1852.
37 C. Mackay, 'Forty Years Recollections of Life, Literature and Public Affairs' in J.G. Read (ed.), *Through Liverpool to North America 1830–1907: A Selection of Emigrant Narratives* (Liverpool: Merseyside Maritime Museum, 1998), pp. 22–3.
38 *Freeman's Journal*, 1 March 1853.
39 National Library of Ireland [hereafter, NLI], MS 41,210, 'Account book of Rev Henry King 1835-50'.
40 *Nenagh Guardian*, 13 April 1853.
41 J.S. Donnelly, *The Land and the People of Nineteenth Century Cork: The Rural Economy and the Land Question* (London: Routledge and Kegan Paul, 1975), p. 108.
42 House of Lords, *Report from the Select Committee of the House of Lords on Colonization from Ireland with Minutes of Evidence, Appendix and Index: Emigration* (London: H.M. Stationery Office, 1847), p. 160.
43 For an overview of the association, see R.J. Purcell, 'The Irish Emigrant Society of New York', *Studies: An Irish Quarterly Review*, 27, 108 (December 1938), pp. 583–99.
44 M.R. Casey, 'Refractive History: Memory and the Founders of the Emigrant Savings Bank' in *Radharc*, 3 (2002), p. 61.
45 See for example, *Nenagh Guardian*, 25 August 1852.
46 *Tuam Herald*, 31 March 1849.
47 *Freeman's Journal*, 27 May 1851.
48 *Belfast Newsletter*, 9 April 1851.
49 *Freeman's Journal*, 26 November 1851.
50 *Belfast Newsletter*, 3 December 1851.
51 See for example, *Irish Examiner*, 29 November 1850.
52 *Freeman's Journal*, 30 December 1851.
53 *Freeman's Journal*, 3 May 1847.
54 *Belfast Newsletter*, 30 March 1847.
55 Ibid. 21 November 1848 and 23 February 1849

56 I am grateful to Edward O'Reilly, Head of the Manuscript Department at the Patricia D. Klingenstein Library, New-York Historical Society, for bringing these papers to my attention and for permission to quote from them.
57 *Freeman's Journal*, 26 November 1851. See also, *Kerry Evening Post*, 13 April 1853.
58 'Minute Book of the Athy Poor Law Union, 16 Sept. 1848', Kildare County Library.
59 'Bell papers', New-York Historical Society.
60 Ibid.
61 *Cork Examiner*, 22 August 1855.
62 Ibid. 2 April 1847.
63 *Kerry Evening Post*, 23 October 1850.
64 S. Barber (ed.), *The Prendergast Letters: Correspondence from Famine-era Ireland, 1840–1850* (Boston: University of Massachusetts Press, 2006), p. 99.
65 *Anglo-Celt*, 27 March 1851.
66 See for example, *Nation*, 15 January 1853.
67 *Freeman's Journal*, 19 August 1854.
68 *Freeman's Journal*, 26 November 1851.
69 *Kerry Evening Post*, 22 January 1853.
70 *Nation*, 20 February 1847.
71 *Cork Examiner*, 4 January 1850.
72 *Freeman's Journal*, 12 April 1853.
73 *Armagh Guardian*, 23 March 1847.
74 T. Anbinder, 'Moving Beyond "Rags to Riches": New York's Irish Famine Immigrants and their Surprising Savings Accounts', *Journal of American History*, 99 (December 2012), pp. 741–70.
75 *Freeman's Journal*, 13 October 1852.
76 *Cork Examiner*, 2 April 1847.

Chapter Eight

Different Writers, Different Perspectives

These very short essays are loosely modelled on the Japanese presentation style known as *pecha kucha* (twenty slides delivered in roughly seven minutes). Contributors approached the challenge from a variety of different perspectives and backgrounds: some are mini versions of traditional presentations whilst others offer something distinctly different.

Singling out any one contribution is always somewhat invidious, but the editors want to say something in particular about Lyn McLeavy's. Lyn's research of her family connects with many of the places, events and themes mentioned elsewhere in this book. Part of her family was from the Cooley peninsula, and they suffered in the Famine, experienced harsh treatment from landlords and were forced to emigrate. Her great-great-grandmother, Jane Cook from Tyrone, suffered the very harshest of conditions on board a prison ship, and afterwards in Van Diemen's Land. Her great-great-grandfather, Owen, was convicted of stealing a cow during the Famine and, being exiled to Bermuda, shared the *Neptune* prison ship with John Mitchel. On landing in Van Diemen's Land, both Owen and John Mitchel were offered conditional pardons. Mitchel got 200 acres and prospered; Owen rented fourteen acres. Later, his early death left Lyn's great-great-grandmother destitute. Lyn, as a representative of huge numbers of family historians whose research traverses the Great Famine, articulates a tone distinctive from that of professional historians but also puts us in touch with an emotional immediacy which is sustained through multiple generations.

We hope readers take something valuable from our *pecha kucha*s.

Seven Famines:
A Hidden Heritage of Hunger

Patrick Fitzgerald

Although few people are likely to contest the proposition that the Great Famine (1845–51) was the greatest calamity in modern Irish and Ulster history, it is still not well understood that it was not unprecedented. Two utterly contrasting publications of 2012 arguably serve to illustrate the point. Tim Pat Coogan's popular conspiracy thesis, *The Famine Plot*, pays very limited attention to Ireland's pre-1845 Famine history. An introductory chronology notes three pre-1845 events, suggesting that the Battle of the Boyne, the 1798 Rebellion and the Act of Union are more germane than any of the numerous and severe mortality crises of the past three centuries. In the proceeding 250-odd pages, 'Ireland's best-known historian' devotes one fleeting paragraph to the original *An Gorta Mór* (The Great Hunger) of 1740–1 and the string of localised famines which characterised the decades before 1845.[1] It is difficult to resist the conclusion that exceptionalism suits the author's flimsy case.[2] Also in 2012, the *Atlas of the Great Irish Famine*, edited by John Crowley, William J. Smyth and Mike Murphy, presented a veritable tour de force by a distinguished team of Ireland's academic historians. However, in a huge work of over 700 pages and almost 90 contributions, only one short five-page essay by David Dickson explicitly addressed earlier Irish famines.[3]

Most people, in fact, seem surprised and even defensive when the primacy of the late 1840s crisis is challenged. In terms of relative excess mortality, the 'Great Famine' was almost certainly third, in Ulster possibly fourth, in the league table of early-modern/modern Irish famines. Between 1500 and the mid-nineteenth century, Ireland experienced no fewer than seven periods of unambiguous famine (1505, 1523–4, 1600–3, 1627–30, 1649–52, 1727–30 and 1740–1) and it is important that we take the longer view of the Great Famine.[4]

Pádraig Lenihan suggests that in the years 1649–52, a lethal cocktail of warfare, plague and famine brought 'countrywide mortality' in the range of 15–20 per cent.[5] David Dickson concludes that the Famine of 1740–1 witnessed excess mortality nationally, estimated at between 13–20 per cent.[6]

This compares with a crude excess mortality rate of just over 12 per cent for the Great Famine.[7] In addition, we might also bear in mind the relative demographic impact of the Irish famine of the late 1720s. Although less calamitous overall than the crisis of 1740–1, this earlier famine was more severe in the northern half of the island. Thus in parts of Ulster it very probably exceeded the mortality rates of both the early 1740s and the late 1840s.[8] Finally, in thinking about poverty, hunger and exposure to the risk of mortality, we should remember the extent to which those in the lowest tier of pre-Famine society found every year a real challenge, rather than in just crisis years. Particularly in the congested districts of the rural west (north and south), the period between June, when the existing potato store became exhausted or inedible, and August, when the fresh crop could be harvested, brought what were popularly referred to as 'the hungry months' or 'meal months'.[9] Even in normal years, when men migrated to find seasonal work and women and children begged, there was no guarantee that ill-health and death could be dodged.

Pulling Back the Veil

Cecil Woodham-Smith's 1962 book *The Great Hunger* remains the most widely read narrative account of the Great Famine but, despite enduring value, it gives the broad impression that the Famine happened in the west of Ireland and that the north of Ireland was essentially different.[10] In fact, our understanding of the geography of the crisis of the late 1840s has been significantly revised in the years since the sesquicentennial commemoration (1995). In Ulster, a useful touchstone for the changed perspective are the conclusions offered by two surveys of the province's economic and social history, published in 1985 and 2013. In 1985, Philip Ollerenshaw concluded that 'North-East Ulster escaped relatively lightly from the Great Famine' whereas in 2013 Liam Kennedy, Kerby Miller and Brian Gurrin suggested that 'the cataclysm of the Great Famine ravaged Ulster'.[11] Thanks to recent research, it is as if a veil has been pulled back on what actually happened in Ulster in the late 1840s.

Exploring one's own family history can sometimes serve to highlight questions of wider importance. In 2013, I visited for the first time the gravestone of my maternal, great-great grandfather, John Harvey, at Tullylish Presbyterian Church near Laurencetown, County Down. Here it is recorded that this Presbyterian smallholding, handloom weaver, from nearby Kernan

Lough, died on 3 December 1846.[12] Though I cannot determine the precise cause of his death, research published since the mid-1990s confirms that had he succumbed to one of the numerous contagious diseases then circulating he would have been far from alone amongst his peers.[13] Today we also know that no fewer than fifty-one Presbyterian ministers in Ulster returned notices to the General Assembly in 1846–7 recording excess mortality amongst their congregations.[14] Furthermore, demographic analysis of the census returns between 1831 and 1861 (encompassing the huge impact of 1845–50) reveals that the decline in the Catholic population of the province (19 per cent) is only very marginally ahead of that amongst the Presbyterian population (18 per cent).[15]

Mitchel and Memory

The strands discussed above, of pre-1845 famines and Ulster Protestant exposure to the worst effects of the Great Famine, are to be seen drawn together in the person of John Mitchel. Rather than seeing Mitchel's Protestant background as appearing exclusively at odds with his views on the Great Famine, might we see his Presbyterian roots as helping to condition a particular sensibility to the effects of dearth? His own father's ancestors were recorded as having crossed from Scotland to Tory Island, off the north-west coast of Donegal, in the turbulent times of the 1680s, when Covenanters were suffering persecution.[16] We should recall, however, that the single greatest surge of migration across the North Channel came in the later 1690s, when departure was conditioned by severe famine in Scotland.[17] As with so many of the stories which attached to Irish-American families who actually left outside the years of the Great Famine, is it possible that the young John Mitchel listened to some family lore which linked the narratives of hunger and migration? Certainly John Mitchel's forebears, who moved on to the area around Dunfanaghy, County Donegal and Dungiven, County Derry, were very likely to have borne, as part of their heritage, the bitter memory of the famines of the late 1720s and early 1740s.[18]

From a Personal Journey to National Commemoration

Michael Blanch

I was born in Ballyfermot and I live in Tallaght. I was a taxi driver, and prior to 1995 and the 150th anniversary of the start of the Great Famine, as I drove visitors around Dublin, the occasional fare would ask about the Famine and I realised there was nothing to show them. Since then there has been a greater awareness as more writers tackled the subject and memorials, like Rowan Gillespie's gaunt Famine Figures on Custom House Quay and the replica *Jeanie Johnson* famine emigration ship, were created. For me it was Ireland's Holocaust, and as I became increasingly aware of the scale and consequences of *An Gorta Mór* I wanted to do something.

In May 2003, my wife Betty and I decided to go down to the site of a soup kitchen[1] at the side of the Four Courts, on Charles Street West, and to walk from there to the docks where people emigrated. There we prayed and shed a tear and I thought that was that, but I kept thinking of the scale of suffering and I knew something more official needed to be done. Our initial meetings involved just family and friends, but as the Committee for the Commemoration of Irish Famine Victims (CCIFV) took shape others came on board, including Pete St John, writer of the Irish folk ballad set during the Great Famine, 'The Fields of Athenry'.

Our main mission was to remember the victims of the Great Famine each year on the second Sunday in May. To this end our first CCIFV walk was held on that day in 2004. We went from the Garden of Remembrance, Parnell Square, down to Custom House Quay. We then realised that if we were to make progress, to involve a much greater number of people, we needed to become more political. We began a campaign, lobbying politicians, both local and national, with a view to establishing a National Great Famine Memorial Day. Pat Rabbitte, the leader of the Labour Party (2002–7), was the first politician to bring us into the Dáil and it was he who asked the all-important first parliamentary question. A series of debates, and much more lobbying, followed until 2008 when the new coalition Government (Fianna Fáil, the Green Party and the Progressive Democrats with the support of some Independents) under Taoiseach Brian Cowan announced on 21 May that the first National Famine Memorial Day would be held on 25 May 2008. This followed an article in the *Sunday Independent* by John O'Keeffe entitled 'President and Others Decline to Attend Famine Memorial Day'.[2]

The Commemoration took place in the Custom House, Dublin and John Curran, the Minister of State (Department of Community, Rural and Gaeltacht Affairs), officiated. It was a small affair held in conjunction with the CCIFV Commemoration Committee mentioned in O'Keeffe's article. It did not receive any media coverage but it is in the Dáil record.[3] However, in July 2008, Éamon Ó Cuív, Minister for Rural, Community and Gaeltacht Affairs, set up the National Famine Commemoration Committee 'to consider ways to commemorate the Irish Famine'.[4] It included historians, Irish language experts and representatives from non-governmental organisations (NGOs).[5] I was also invited to join.

This first National Famine Commemoration Committee organised the second National Famine Commemoration, in Skibbereen, on Sunday 17 May 2009.[6] The main features were the involvement of religious leaders, ambassadors to Ireland and the Irish Army. The commemoration would also involve one or two weeks of community reflection with Famine walks, drama, art, music, lectures, re-enactments etc. The Committee proposed that the annual commemoration would be rotated clockwise around the provinces. The Committee also initiated recognition of the diaspora by having an international commemoration of the Great Famine. The first of those was in Grosse Isle, Canada, where on Sunday, 10 May 2009 minister Éamon Ó Cuív declared: 'This is truly a most special and poignant place – sacred in many ways. Indeed, I am delighted that Grosse Ile is the location that was selected as the first overseas location for the commemoration of the Great Irish Famine'.[7] Table 1 shows the location of all the Commemorations, both national and international, up until 2016.

After serving two years on the National Famine Commemoration Committee I was not reappointed, but along with the CCIFV I have continued to lobby enthusiastically – this time to have the National Famine Commemoration on a set date. We suggested the second Sunday in May, which I felt would further emphasise the importance of the day and acknowledge the suffering of our people. It would put the National Famine Commemoration Day on a par with St Patrick's Day and the commemoration of the Easter Rising. It would also allow the President to make arrangements always to attend. There was opposition within government,[8] but I am delighted to record that due to the efforts of TDs Colm Brophy (Fine

Table 1. National and International Famine Commemorations, 2008–16

Year	National Venue	International Venue
2008	Custom House, Co. Dublin	
2009	Skibbereen, Co. Cork	Grosse Isle, Canada
2010	Murrisk, Co. Mayo	New York City, USA
2011	Clones, Co. Monaghan	Liverpool, England
2012	Drogheda, Co. Louth	Boston, USA
2013	Kilrush, Co. Clare	Sydney, Australia
2014	Strokestown, Co. Roscommon	New Orleans, USA
2015	Newry, Co. Down	Saint John, New Brunswick, Canada
2016	Glasnevin, Co. Dublin	Philadelphia, USA

Gael) and previously Peadar Tóibín (Sinn Féin), in February 2017 a private member's bill, supported by the government, passed the second stage in the Dáil.[9]

In 2015, following six years, intensive lobbying, north and south, by Anthony Russell and the Newry and Mourne District Council's Great Famine Commemoration Committee, the Famine commemoration crossed the border.[10] It had nearly happened once before, in 2011 in Clones, but it was eventually held in the North, and very successfully. In July 2014, both Jim Wells of the Democratic Unionist Party and Danny Kennedy of the Ulster Unionist Party wrote to the Sinn Féin Culture Arts and Leisure Minister, Carál Ní Chuilín, in support of the famine commemoration crossing the border (see p. 128).

On this occasion the Irish Army did not participate, and on other occasions either the Taoiseach or the President attended, though neither was present in Newry. Martin McGuiness, Deputy First Minister, represented the government of Northern Ireland and Heather Humphreys, Minister for Arts, Heritage, Regional, Rural and Gaeltacht Affairs, represented the Irish government. The commemoration in Newry helped challenge the popular view that Ulster was not affected by the Famine, yet we shared mass graves, as on the Shankill Road, in Belfast,[11] and we were lost together at sea.

I am an activist who believes that the Great Famine, and the destitution it caused, has until recently suffered from suppression by omission.

Department of
Culture, Arts
and Leisure
www.dcalni.gov.uk
AN ROINN
Cultúir, Ealaíon
agus Fóillíochta
MÄNNYSTRIE O
Fowkgates, Airts
an Aisedom

Causeway Exchange
1-7 Bedford Street
Belfast BT2 7EG
Tel: +44 (0) 28 9025 8825
Text phone: (0) 28 9052 7668
email: dcalni@dcalni.gov.uk

Date: **17 July 2014**
Our Ref: **SECCOR152/2014**

Jim Wells MLA
Parliament Buildings
Ballymiscaw
Stormont
BELFAST
BT4 3XX

Dear Mr Wells

2015 NATIONAL FAMINE COMMEMORATION

Thank you for your correspondence of 26th June 2014 regarding contact made by Anthony Russell, Historian in relation to the 2015 National Famine Commemoration.

I can advise you that Minister Ní Chuilín is supportive of Mr Russell's proposals for the 2015 National Famine Commemorations to be held in Newry.

Minister Ní Chuilín will also be meeting with Mr Russell on 30 July 2014 to discuss further, plans for the 2015 National Famine Commemoration.

Yours sincerely

PETER MAY
Interim Permanent Secretary

INVESTORS IN PEOPLE

A confident, creative, informed and healthy society

Unfortunately, this extends to our National Museum. There is national amnesia in our National Museum – where in the museum are the stories and the artefacts from An Gorta Mór? CCIFV has met with politicians and representatives of the National Museum to lobby to have a room dedicated to, in my opinion, the most important event in Irish history. There have been vague promises and expressions of interest but, as yet, no practical results.

This chapter is a personal reflection on a campaign to establish a National Famine Memorial Day. I am proud of what the CCIFV has achieved and I am pleased that the most important period in our shared history will have a permanent date in the calendar and the suffering of millions will not be forgotten, at home or abroad.

Mitchel and Slavery: A Biblical Perspective

Revd Nigel Agnew

There are very few individuals in history who have made undertakings that are simply intended to be of academic interest to succeeding generations. Rather, they do things out of a sense of justice, and no matter whether we agree with them or not, those famous words attributed to Mitchel regarding the Almighty, the English and the Famine were surely written out of a sense of justice. Yet, some might ask, where was that same sense of justice when it came to supporting slavery in America? Some theological arguments, written by American theologians in the mid-nineteenth century (with whom Mitchel may have had some contact), might even have given Mitchel some further justification for his views on slavery. Yet, the question is: 'Does the Bible lay down an absolute standard in relation to slavery?' Does it state this standard explicitly? Or is it more subtle?

Most of the Bible was written at a time when slavery was a common feature of many cultures and societies. One of the relevant dates in the Old Testament is the giving of the law to Moses at Mount Sinai, which took place around 1400 BC. Before that it seems that other societies regulated slavery – for example, the Hammurabi Code originating in Mesopotamia (around 1750 BC) is evidence for this and the book of Job, probably written before 1400 BC, mentions that slaves had certain rights. The Law of Moses regulated many things in life, which included slavery for Jews and non-Jews. Non-Jewish slaves were allowed to participate in certain Jewish festivals and rituals and they did not work on the Jewish Sabbath. Slave owners would be punished if they beat a slave to death (Exodus 21:20). However, most of the slavery we read about in the Old Testament was that of Jewish people. Often this would have arisen out of economic necessity, and there are certain themes that must be stressed about such slavery:

> **First, slavery was never meant to be permanent.** It was always meant to be temporary. Slaves were to be released after serving six years, (Deuteronomy 15:12–15) and the seventh-year release was to be observed by all.
>
> **Secondly, a Jewish slave owner was to treat his Jewish slave in a particular way.** He was to ensure that there was no harsh treatment and

the subject was to be treated more like a hired servant than a slave. Each Jew was to think about slavery and freedom in a unique way.

What was behind this thinking? We get some idea from Deuteronomy 15: 15, which mentions the Exodus from Egypt. The Jewish people went into Egypt as a large family around 1850 BC because of famine, yet they went as free people. They came out of Egypt about 400 years later as a nation, but only after being enslaved. In Deuteronomy 15:15 they were to remember this time of slavery and they were to remember that they had been liberated from slavery. It was to affect the way they treated one another. The Exodus liberation from slavery is portrayed as God going to great lengths to liberate his people. The word 'Redemption' sums it all up; God has paid a price to set his people free. This was symbolised through the sacrifice of a first-born lamb. Consequently, if the people were set free by God the ultimate ideal could not be to enslave one another. Rather, the ultimate goal was to be free, which is why every seven years, freedom was remembered, and this attitude was to permeate society.

In the New Testament era there was a different attitude to slavery. Many had followed Greek thought in considering that some people were 'natural slaves', and many thought that certain people needed to be ruled over for their own good. It would be hard to generalise and say that we know what the life of a typical slave was like in the first century. Yet some slaves could buy their own freedom and this idea of being 'redeemed' is used by the apostle Paul to describe what the gospel is about. The Greek word for 'redemption' is a word that was used for a slave being liberated by the payment of a price. Paul probably deliberately uses this in Romans 3:24 ('They are justified freely by His grace through the redemption that is in Christ Jesus'). Thus, for Paul, redemption primarily means that people are liberated from sin by Jesus.

The apostles also gave practical advice on the issue of slavery. To understand this we must be aware of the existence in the first century of what are called 'household codes'. These codes were important to Aristotle and many others, for they were foundational for the proper ordering of society. The essential features are that society is made up of three sets of relationships: namely, master and slave, husband and wife, parents and children. In each case one rules and the other is ruled over. So when we look at the teaching of the apostles we might expect to see an explicit view on slavery itself. However, all we actually see is Peter simply telling Christian slaves to be good. He tells them to work for their owners even if they are treated harshly (1 Peter 2:18–21). Peter seems to follow the structure of the household codes, yet we also see that he asks people to take a new look at these household codes in light of Christianity. Thus he did not advance detailed theories towards how Christian slaves should seek liberation.

Paul approached slavery in a similar way to that of Peter. He also tells the Christian slave owners to behave in a certain way (Ephesians 6:9), and the lack of an explicit scriptural condemnation of slavery led many to conclude that slavery should be tolerated in America. However, it seems a little more subtle than that. Paul wrote to a man called Philemon, a slave owner, about his runaway slave, Onesimus. Paul met Onesimus and is sending him back to Philemon, but Philemon is a Christian and Paul ensures that the whole situation is considered through the central tenets of the Christian faith. In Philemon 1:15–19, we read:

> For perhaps he was for this reason parted from you for a while, that you should have him back forever, no longer as a slave, but more than a slave, a beloved brother, especially to me, but how much more to you, both in the flesh and in the Lord. If then you regard me a partner, accept him as you would me. But if he has wronged you in any way, or owes you anything, charge that to my account; I, Paul, am writing this with my own hand, I will repay it (lest I should mention to you that you owe to me even your own self as well).

Philemon would remember that at the very centre of Christianity is the idea that sins are transferred from the believer to Christ. This should be worked out in how Philemon viewed Paul and Onesimus, and in a sense words such as this should 'embarrass' Christian slave owners into re-evaluating slavery.

In summary, the Bible speaks in a more subtle way against slavery. It shows that a society with redemption at its centre has no real room for slavery. I think this was either overlooked or ignored by many in nineteenth-century America. Yet, thankfully, some realised that in a land where many claimed to follow the Bible slavery could not continue.

Newry Workhouse

Hugh McShane

On 3 May 1839, the Newry Poor Law Union was created, one of 130 being established throughout Ireland. It was novel that its 215 square miles, with a population of 88,181 in twenty-three electoral divisions,[1] did not recognise existing county, barony or parish boundaries. For example, Table 1 shows both Newry (10,004) and Ballybot (5,831). Ballybot, in County Armagh, was part of the urban fabric of Newry but being in another county it had its own courthouse and bridewell. However, along with the County Down part of Newry it was incorporated into the Newry Union.[2] This new administrative area was controlled by a Board of forty-one Guardians, ten of whom were ex-officio and thirty-one who were identified with specific areas.

Near the centre of each union in Ireland was the workhouse, and since all workhouses were situated 'in or near a market town',[3] Newry was a logical choice. A site on high ground at Daisy Hill to the east of the town was chosen. The Newry Workhouse was contracted on 17 December 1839 and the first inmates entered the purpose-built workhouse on 16 December 1841. Among those admitted in the first few weeks were the paupers of the recently closed Newry Workhouse and Mendicity Association.[4]

The workhouse, with a capacity for 1,000 inmates, was to George Wilkinson's standard plan. The Newry Granite for the building was taken from a nearby quarry which also was the source of clean water. As elsewhere, the regime was associated with 'despondency and social humiliation' and with 'forced separation of families, cramped and regimented living conditions and strict tests of admission which were meant to discourage entry except for the most desperate of cases'.[5] Whether because of the relative prosperity of Newry and its hinterland, or the success of the strict regime in repelling people, numbers generally remained below capacity, so much so that in 1842 William Makepeace Thackeray could write: 'The Newry poor-house is as neatly ordered and comfortable as any house, public or private, in Ireland; the same look of health which was so pleasant to see among the Naas children of the union-house was to be remarked here; the same care and comfort for the old people'.[6] In October 1845, there were 351 pauper inmates;[7] however, as described elsewhere in this book, had Thackeray's visit taken place between 1846 and 1850 he would have witnessed across the Union a scene transformed

Table 1. Newry Union: Counties, electoral divisions, population and number of guardians

County	Electoral Division	Population	Number of Guardians
Down	Newry	10,004	4
Down	Ouley	2,974	1
Down	Crobane	3,601	1
Down	Donaghmore	2,378	1
Down	Glen	2,985	1
Down	Warrenpoint	4,125	2
Down	U. Clonallon	4,053	1
Down	Rathfriland	4,419	2
Down	Drumgath	2,683	1
Down	Hilltown	2,457	1
Down	Clonduff	3,320	1
Armagh	Ballybot	5,831	2
Armagh	Mullaghglass	2,294	1
Armagh	Poyntzpass	5,331	2
Armagh	Mountnorris	3,257	1
Armagh	Belleek	3,193	1
Armagh	Tullyhappy	3,133	1
Armagh	Ballymoyer	2,729	1
Armagh	Jonesborough	3,972	1
Armagh	Killeavy	4,199	1
Armagh	Camlough	4,572	2
Armagh	Forkhill	3,851	1
Armagh	Latbirget	2,921	1

Note: Ballybot is part of Newry Town. There were also ten ex-officio guardians.

by the failure of the potato and the destitution of the small tenant farmer, the cottier and the labourer. In contrast to Thackery's observations, in February 1847, there were forty-two deaths in one week.[8]

For his efforts, tending the sick for over thirty-six years in Newry Workhouse, Dr William Alexander Davis earned praise and a tablet commending his practice in St Mary's Church of Ireland, Newry. At the height of the Great Famine in 1847, Dr Davis caught the fever,[9] but even though other officers died of the disease, he returned to work. Reports for 1849, following the impact of the failure of the potato in the Newry area, tell of the workhouse returning to normal. There is reference to trying to reduce any tension between the inmates and the town: 'Intercourse, as far as possible, between the town and the inmates should be cut off by the disallowance of passes and … the greatest attention should be paid to cleanliness, arm clothing and ventilation in the house'.[10] Perhaps a strange statement given that the prevailing philosophy was to make the workhouse an unattractive place; to keep people out rather than in.

The general improvement in workhouses in Ireland after the famine was noted by Sir John Forbes who, in *Memorandums Made in Ireland in the Autumn of 1852*, commented: 'Except [for] the police barracks, nothing domestic in all Ireland struck me more than the neatness and cleanliness

Table 2. Types of work in Newry Workhouse, February 1849

Female	**Number**	**Male**	**Number**
Picking oakum	74	Field labouring	26
Sewing and knitting	50	Carpentry	2
Veining muslin	90	Whitewashing	5
Laundry	20	Plastering	2
Kitchen	20	Graveyard	2
Yard-sweeping	6	Watchmen	3
Nursing infants	51	Carrying milk	2
Attending children	30	Cutting oakam	2
Attending female idiots	2	Tailoring	21
		Shoemaking	21

of these houses'.[11] The minutes of the Guardians, justly or otherwise, take pride in the workhouse: 'There is probably not a house in Ireland where, out of such a large number, there are so few sick and so few deaths'.[12] Even in the winter of 1850, as the cold weather drove greater numbers into the house – 108 in one day, suffering from cold and hunger – Mr Barron, the inspector, still picked up on the improvement: 'I think it right to state that the workhouse and the hospital are by far better than they were on my previous inspection'.[13]

Examples of the work done by the inmates[14] is set out, according to gender, in Table 2. Much of the work, like yard-sweeping, whitewashing, looking after children or grave digging, was related to the upkeep of the house.

Newry Workhouse survived until 1948 when, with the creation of the National Health Service, which ended the poor law system north of the border, it became Daisy Hill Hospital.

The Irish National Famine Museum: Strokestown Park

John O'Driscoll

Strokestown, County Roscommon, is an Irish estate town famed for many things, one of which is, allegedly, Ireland's widest street. Strokestown was home to the Mahon family from the mid-1600s until 1981, and very importantly was the residence of Major Denis Mahon, the first landlord assassinated during the Great Irish Famine. Now home to the Irish National Famine Museum, as one looks straight down the main street of Strokestown one can see the triple-arched neo-gothic entrance to the Strokestown Estate. A very definite separation between town and estate.

In 1979, Jim Callery purchased the Strokestown estate to accommodate his new Scania truck dealership. At the time Jim did not have enough land around the garage premises to accommodate his new dealership, and wanted to buy about three or four acres of the estate. The Pakenham Mahon family were not keen to see the estate get any smaller, as it had been in excess of 30,000 acres in the mid-nineteenth century and was by then reduced to a little over 300 acres. However, when the estate went up for auction Jim Callery succeeded in purchasing the lot. Shortly after purchasing the estate, the Strokestown archive came to light and in particular the Cloonahee Petition was discovered, a petition asking for Famine relief work from the tenants of the townland where Jim Callery grew up and where he still lives today. This changed everything and led to the start of one of the largest privately funded restoration projects to take place in Ireland.

The renowned Strokestown Park Archive contains in excess of 50,000 documents, which throw light on estate life from the early 1800s right through to the mid-twentieth century. The continuous story of the estate through the Great Irish Famine, comprising of emigration lists, landlord–agent correspondence, eviction notices and much more is revealed. Details of Major Mahon's emigration scheme are also contained within the documents. The archive is housed in what was once the estate office, using best conservation practices. An international Archive Advisory Committee has been set up to look at the Archive, to make sure that it is cared for and to enhance its availability for study purposes. The first initiative has been coordinated already with the help of Dr Danielle O'Donovan of the Irish Heritage Trust and Trinity College Dublin: Great Famine Voices (www.greatfaminevoices.ie), seeking out the lived experience of the Great Hunger on the ground across Ireland. This was launched during Heritage week 2015 and is growing rapidly with fresh stories coming in every few days.

The Cloonahee Petition is a really good example of the kind of document held by the Archive. On 22 August 1846, the tenants of the townland of Cloonahee near Elphin, County Roscommon, wrote to their landlord asking for famine relief. It seems that the relief works had stopped in the area leaving the people with nothing. They write: 'Our Families are really and truly suffering in our presence and we cannot much longer withstand their cries for food'. The wording in this document takes on an interesting tone when they further write: 'We are not for joining in anything illegal or contrary to the laws of God or the Land unless pressed to by HUNGER'. We must note that the word 'hunger' is written in capital letters in the document.

Major Denis Mahon had inherited the Strokestown estate in 1845 and it was clearly a debt-ridden estate at the beginning of the Great Irish Famine. John Ross Mahon was brought in as an advisor, and in a document on display in the Famine Museum, John Ross advises Major Mahon: 'Emigration on an extensive Scale is the principle feature in my plan'. Too many tenants on the estate were never going to be in a position to pay rent and this was seen as unsustainable. The Major took up the advice of John Ross Mahon and put into action a scheme for the assisted emigration of 1,490 people, walking them along the Royal Canal to Dublin, and from there shipping them to Liverpool and then onto Quebec. An eviction scheme was also put into practice in 1847 and in excess of 3,000 people were evicted from the estate. In November 1847, Major Mahon was assassinated in the townland of Doorty, just outside the boundary of his estate.

His Archive lives on in Strokestown Park and the Irish National Famine Museum today uses these documents to commemorate the Great Irish Famine. The Museum opened in 1994 and is housed in what were once the farm buildings of the estate, ironically sitting in the shadow of the 'Big House'. President Mary Robinson was the first Patron of the Famine Museum and on the opening day she expressed the view that: 'This Famine Museum shows us that history is not about power and triumph nearly so often as it is about suffering and vulnerability'. The Patronage was continued by President Mary McAleese and President Michael D. Higgins, who remains a Patron of the Famine Museum today. Comprising ten rooms and drawing on the

Strokestown Archive, the museum aims to commemorate and to discuss the circumstances of the Great Irish Famine. In excess of 50,000 visitors pass through the museum each year and it continues to enlighten and interest both national and international audiences.

When visiting Strokestown Park one is given an insight into the faded grandeur of Ascendancy Ireland and also the harrowing story of the tenants during the Great Irish Famine. As well as commemorating the Great Irish Famine, the Famine Museum in Strokestown attempts to draw parallels with contemporary global issues of hunger and deprivation. If the Famine Museum can do its part in raising awareness of the history of the Great Irish Famine, while reminding people that world hunger and mass human migration continue, then something valuable has been achieved. Helping people consider our past and take action today can, one hopes, make a lasting contribution.

An Australian Famine Family

Lyn McLeavy

Editors' Note

Lyn's research of her family connects with many of the places, events and themes mentioned elsewhere in this book. Part of her family was from the Cooley Peninsula, a hilly region in County Louth. They suffered in the Famine, experienced harsh treatment from landlords and were assisted or forced to emigrate. There is mention in the folk memory of starvation and proselytising.

Lyn's great-great-grandmother, Jane Cook from Tyrone, suffered the very harshest conditions on board a prison ship, and afterwards in Van Diemen's Land. Her great-great-grandfather, Owen, convicted of stealing a cow during the Famine and being exiled to Bermuda, shared the prison ship Neptune with John Mitchel. On landing in Van Dieman's Land, both Owen and John Mitchel were offered conditional pardons. Mitchel received 200 acres and prospered, while Owen rented fourteen acres. His early death left Lyn's great-great-grandmother destitute. This is her story.

When the Great Famine began my great-great-grandmother, Jane Cook, was twenty-one. Her daughter, Ann Young, was five and there was also a younger child. Jane's husband, William Young, seems to have died during the course of the crisis.[1] Before August 1848, Jane had already been imprisoned in Omagh, County Tyrone, twice: three months 'for meat'; then twelve months 'for leaving my child'.[2] She then began to suffer what were described as 'hysterical fits'.[3] In October 1849, Jane was convicted of stealing a pot lid and sentenced to ten years' transportation.[4] Grangegorman Prison, Dublin, recorded her as literate with no occupation and noted her 'good behaviour'.[5]

Two hundred women and thirty-two children were 'disposed of' on the *Duke of Cornwall* in July 1850 to Van Diemen's Land.[6] Many of them, including Jane, suffered hysteria and she is recorded as being hospitalised for three weeks and treated by being burned, bled and having vinegar and water poured from a height onto her shaved scalp.[7]

Arriving in Hobart, the ship's matron initiated an inquiry into sexual misconduct by the officers and crew, which found 'great irregularities', and those in charge were condemned as 'unfit for so important a charge'.[8] At disembarkation, Jane said she was a widow and laundress (and had a brother in Philadelphia).[9] She was sent to Brickfields Hiring Depot for a year and a half, then into service at Franklin in the Huon Valley,[10] an Irish settlement in what was a very Anglo-Saxon colony.[11] Jane's daughter, Ann, was sent to the Queen's Orphan Asylum in Hobart, a cold hell in which few people had much interest, where early death was a common feature.[12] Matron Smyth, a sadist with a dog that bit children, was in charge and the Reverend attached to the asylum had already been tried and reprimanded for sexual misconduct.[13] Ann had the great misfortune to become his servant.[14]

Six months after arriving in Hobart, Jane went 'absent' and was punished with fourteen days' hard labour at the Female Factory,[15] a prison in a damp, low-lying, sunless valley known as the 'Shadow of Death Valley' – reflecting the numbers of women and children who went to early graves there.[16] Soon after she received a further month's hard labour for being drunk. Two months after arriving in Franklin, she married Owen O'Connor.[17]

***

In January 1848, my great-great-grandfather, Owen O'Connor of Tralee, County Kerry, was a 31-year-old widower who had stolen a cow at the height of the Famine. Along with his two brothers, 20-year-old Cornelius and 38-year-old Thomas, he was sentenced to ten years' transportation to Bermuda.[18] There they worked at the British Naval Dockyard for fifteen months then, selected for good health and conduct, they were sent with some 293 other convicts, including John Mitchel, the Irish Nationalist lawyer charged with treason, to South Africa on the *Neptune*.[19] On arrival, the *Neptune* was refused landing by Anti-Transportationists.[20] They were at sea for a full year and up to eighteen of those on board died whilst others mutinied.[21]

They were finally released in Hobart in April 1850, and Owen and his brothers were issued with Conditional Pardons.[22] Owen went to Franklin where he took up farming, whilst his brothers apparently disappeared from the historical record. Back in Ireland the family mostly vanished from Tralee, but Owen's son is recorded as getting married there in 1859.[23]

Jane and Owen rented fourteen acres[24] and had three daughters, the middle one my great-grandmother, Johanna.[25] Owen died aged fifty-three of 'paralysis' (a stroke) in May 1871[26] and is buried in an unmarked grave. After his death Jane became homeless and destitute. She was charged with 'sleeping in an outhouse', and described as a 'widow – being an idle and disorderly person wandering abroad, having no fixed abode and no visible means of support' (one month hard labour); stealing meat (one year hard labour); stealing a pair of boots (six months);[27] 'a suspected person found in possession of certain copper coins' (one month hard labour).[28] Johanna, my great-grandmother, was fourteen years old at Owen's death and she went to Melbourne, escaping the punishing place that was Tasmania.[29] Her sisters disappeared from history.

Jane was sentenced to the Female Factory a remarkable thirty-seven times, mostly for being drunk, once for disturbing the peace and uttering obscene language and three times for idle and disorderly behaviour. Finding herself unable to pay fines of between five shillings and three pounds, she did nearly three years' hard labour at cold outdoor washtubs on an inadequate diet and endured a total of five weeks' solitary confinement in soundproof and lightproof cells, subsisting on bread and water.[30] Jane died aged sixty-six, a servant at the New Town Charitable Institution, 'of heart disease'[31] and is buried in an unmarked 'pauper's grave'.[32]

***

The McAleavys had been farming in the townland of Drummullagh, on the Anglesey Estate on the Louth shore of Carlingford Lough, since 1760,[33] with rent set at £18 2s 6d[34] and in 1769 a 31-year lease.[35] In 1784, they held 12 acres, 27 perches for a rental of £8 9s 7d.[36] In the years after the potato blight struck in the autumn of 1845 we can see glimpses of how life deteriorated in Drummullagh.

In June 1846, Lord Anglesey's agent bought fifteen and a half tons of oatmeal and Indian meal 'for tenants in want of food'. Sickness was reported and road building relief works were undertaken. People were ejected, houses destroyed, and sons and daughters were 'assisted to America'.[37]

> October: Absentee landlord, the Marquess of Anglesey – hero of Waterloo, twice Lord Lieutenant of Ireland, Head of British Ordnance and one of the richest men in Britain – replied to the agent's recommendation of 20 per cent reduction in rent by stating 'non-payment of rent ... will never be permitted ... exact repayment in labour, for every advance of money or food'.[38]

Lord Anglesey's son, a notorious gambler, fled to England on a £200 a year allowance, when he could have been transported for fraud.[39]

My great-great-grandparents, 50-year-old Hugh McAleavey and Sarah McCaherty, took a boat to the relatively nearby haven of Douglas, Isle of Man with their children Mary (16), Barney (13), and my great-grandfather Ardil, aged just nine, where they remained until they died in 1871.[40] A 12-year-old eyewitness from Omeath reportedly commented that 'people died from hunger, but not many, the shore saved them. They lived mainly on mussels ... there were dead people and no-one to bury them ... everyone was afraid to go near a house where people had died'.[41]

1847: A famine pot on the shore was allegedly provided by proselytising agents.[42] Lord Anglesey called for more money for the military rather than relief in Ireland.[43]

1848: McCaherty family 'ejected' – Anglesey 'lost £5-2s-2d'.[44]

1849: 'Two pounds lost, by widow McEleavey ejected, to assist her going to America, arrears unpaid £2-5s-9d'. (I believe this may have been the then very old Rose McAleavy.)[45]

1850: Hugh McEleavy 'surrenders'. One pound lost. Arrears £2-10s-0d.[46] Local newspaper reports mass evictions.[47]

1851: Land surveyed, guns provided for bailiffs, dogs shot. Poor children provided with clothes.[48]

1852: Anglesey, known for liberal hospitality at his various mansions, organised shooting parties three days a week.[49]

1853: Hugh and James McAleavy ejected from five acres.[50]

Reflections

It was time-consuming and difficult finding my Irish story, the treasure of my life, but it has proved a rewarding experience. Clearly, Jane's many imprisonments for being drunk revealed a trauma from a hard life she did not deserve. Too much loss, suffering and persecution were endured and, like Jane, so many Irish ended up in institutions in Australia. The experience of losing family, home, culture, language and country parallels what still happens to Australian Aborigines today. There is no shame in stealing food and becoming 'a convict' when you are being starved.

Notes

Patrick Fitzgerald

1 T.P. Coogan, *The Famine Plot: England's Role in Ireland's Greatest Tragedy* (Basingstoke: Palgrave Macmillan, 2012), pp. ix, 14.

2 For an elaboration of the critique, see Peter Gray's review of the book under the heading 'Polemic without plausibility' *Irish Times*, 19 January 2013: irishtimes.com/culture/books/polemic-without-plausibility-1.963743 (accessed 10 May 2017).

3 D. Dickson, '1740–41 Famine' in J. Crowley, W.J. Smyth and M. Murphy (eds), *Atlas of the Great Irish Famine* (Cork: Cork University Press, 2012), pp. 23–7.

4 E.M. Crawford (ed.), *Famine: The Irish Experience 900–1900* (Edinburgh: J. Donald, 1989), pp. 97, 226.

5 P. Lenihan, 'War and Population, 1649–52' in *Irish Economic and Social History*, 24, (1997), p. 19.

6 D. Dickson, *Arctic Ireland: The Extraordinary Story of the Great Frost and Forgotten Famine of 1740–41* (Belfast: White Row Press, 1997), p. 69.

7 This figure is arrived at simply by expressing the broadly accepted excess mortality estimate of 1 million deaths as a proportion of the 1841 census population estimate of 8,175,124.

8 D. Dickson, 'The Gap in Famines: A Useful Myth?' in Crawford, *Famine*, p. 97; J. Kelly, 'Harvests and Hardship: Famine and Scarcity in Ireland in the late 1720s', *Studia Hibernica*, 26, (1992), pp. 65–105.

9 J. Percival, *The Great Famine: Ireland's Potato Famine, 1845–1851* (London: Book Club Associates, 1995), pp. 38, 63.

10 C. Woodham-Smith, *The Great Hunger* (London: Old Town Books, 1962), p. 14. Whilst the author offers some differentiation between regions within the province there remains little scope for the crisis impacting upon Ulster Protestants.

11 P. Ollerenshaw, 'Industry, 1820–1914' in L. Kennedy and P. Ollerenshaw (eds.), *An Economic History of Ulster, 1820–1939* (Manchester: Manchester University Press, 1985), p. 74; L. Kennedy, K.A. Miller and B. Gurrin, 'People and Population Change, 1600–1914' in L. Kennedy and P. Ollerenshaw (eds), *Ulster Since 1600: Politics, Economy and Society* (Oxford: Oxford University Press, 2013), p. 66.

12 Also recorded in R.S.J. Clarke (ed.), *The Heart of Downe: Old Banbridge Families from Gravestone Inscriptions, Wills and Biographical Notes* (Belfast: Ulster Historical Foundation, 1989), p. 146.

13 M. Cohen, *Linen, Family and Community in Tullylish, County Down 1690–1914* (Dublin: Four Courts Press, 1997), p. 155; G. Mac Atasney, *'This Dreadful Visitation': The Famine in Lurgan/Portadown* (Dublin: Beyond the Pale, 1997), p. 111.

14 D.W. Miller, 'Irish Presbyterians and the Great Famine' in J. Hill and C. Lennon (eds), *Luxury and Austerity* (Dublin: University College Dublin Press, 1999), pp. 166–7.

15 K.A. Miller, B. Gurrin and L. Kennedy, 'The Great Famine and Religious Demography in Mid-Nineteenth-Century Ulster' in Crowley, Smyth and Murphy, *Atlas of the Great Irish Famine*, p. 429.

16 W. Dillon, *Life of John Mitchel*, vol. 1 (London: Kegan Paul, Trench & Co., 1888), pp. 2–3.

17 K.J. Cullen, *Famine in Scotland: The 'Ill Years' of the 1690s* (Edinburgh: Edinburgh University Press, 2010), pp. 157–86; P. Fitzgerald, '"Black' 97": Reconsidering Scottish

Migration to Ireland in the Seventeenth Century and the Scotch-Irish in America', in W. Kelly and J.R. Young (eds), *Ulster and Scotland, 1600–2000: History, Language and Identity* (Dublin: Four Courts Press, 2004), pp. 71–84.

18 Dillon, *John Mitchel*, pp. 2–3; A.G. Russell, *Between Two Flags: John Mitchel & Jenny Verner* (Dublin: Merrion Press, 2015), p. 5.

Michael Blanch

1 E. Delaney, *The Great Irish Famine – A History in Four Lives* (Dublin: Gill and Macmillan, 2014).
2 *Sunday Independent*, 18 May 2008.
3 House of the Oireachtas: http://oireachtasdebates.oireachtas.ie/debates%20authoring/debateswebpack.nsf/takes/dail2016112900087 (accessed 21 April 2017).
4 *Irish Times*, 22 July 2008.
5 Ibid.
6 *Irish Examiner*, 8 January 2009.
7 Éamon Ó Cuív, an address at Grosse Isle on 10 May 2009: www.irishfamine.ie/wp-content/uploads/2015/11/2009-05-13-FINAL-speech-for-Grosse-Ile-Quebec.pdf (accessed 21 April 2017).
8 'Calls for a Fixed Date in the Year to Remember Ireland's Great Famine', *The Journal*, 8 July 2016: www.thejournal.ie/politicians-asking-for-fixed-date-great-famine-commemorations-2866376-Jul2016/ (accessed 21 April 2017).
9 M. O'Halloran, 'Minister Questions Military Element of Famine Commemoration', *Irish Times*, 21 February 2017: www.irishtimes.com/news/politics/oireachtas/minister-questions-military-element-of-famine-commemoration-1.2984237 (accessed 10 May 2017).
10 B. Campbell, 'Thousands Attend North's First Famine Commemoration Ceremony' *Irish News*, 28 September 2015: www.irishnews.com/news/northernirelandnews/2015/09/28/news/thousands-attend-north-s-first-famine-commemoration-ceremony-274889/ (accessed 10 May 2017).
11 *Belfast News Letter*, 6 August 2015.

Hugh McShane

1 M.H. Gould, *The Workhouses of Ulster* (Belfast: Ulster Architecture Heritage Society, 1983).
2 'The Workhouse: The Story of an Institution, Newry, Co. Down': www.workhouses.org.uk/Newry/ (accessed 21 April 2017).
3 C. Kinealy, 'The Administration of the Irish Poor Law 1838-62,' unpublished PhD thesis, Trinity College Dublin (1984).
4 Newry, Mourne and Down District Council, 'The Workhouse during the Famine': www.newrymournedown.org/the_workhouse_during_the_famine (accessed 21 April 2017).
5 E.M. Fitzgerald, *Commemorating the Irish Famine* (Liverpool: Liverpool University Press, 2013), p. 103.
6 W.M. Thackeray, *The Irish Sketchbook*, vol. 1 (London: Smith, Elder & Co., 1903), p. 335.
7 *Newry Commercial Telegraph*, 31 October 1845.

8 Ibid. 19 February 1847.
9 Ibid. 27 February 1847.
10 Ibid. 27 February 1849.
11 J. Forbes, *Memorandums Made in Ireland in the Autumn of 1852,* vol. 1 (London: Smith, Elder & Co., 1853), p. 279.
12 *Newry Commercial Telegraph,* 18 December 1849.
13 Ibid. 29 January 1850.
14 Ibid. 27 February 1849.

Lyn McLeavy

1 Tasmanian Archive and Heritage Office [hereafter, TAHO], CON41/1/28; 'Conduct Registers of Female Convicts Arriving in the Period of the Probation System, 1 January 1844 to 31 December 1853'; 'Conduct Record for Jane Cook, Duke of Cornwall, 8 July to 27 October 1850'.
2 Ibid.
3 TAHO, ADM101/20, Reel 3192: 'Surgeon's Journal of Duke of Cornwall, 5 July to 4 November 1850': www.femaleconvicts.org.au/docs/ships/SurgeonsJournal_DukeOfCornwall1850.pdf (accessed 22 April 2017).
4 TAHO, CON41/1/28.
5 National Archive of Ireland [hereafter, NAI], 'Register of Female Convicts held at Grangegorman Prison, Dublin, 11 July 1840 to 22 December 1853'.
6 NAI, Miscellaneous/6/1850, 'Letter from Convict Department of Office of Chief Secretary for Ireland, 9 May 1850'.
7 TAHO, 'Surgeon's Journal'.
8 State Library of New South Wales [hereafter, SLNSW], Tasmanian Papers 112, 20567-24010, Convict Department: 'Letters received 1851 to 1864, 22 November 1851'.
9 TAHO, CON41/1/28.
10 Ibid.
11 Richard Davis: www.utas.edu.au/library/companion to tasmanian history/E/Exile p.3 (1 Sept. 2015).
12 J. Purtscher, *Children in Queen's Orphanages, Hobart Town, 1828–1863* (Hobart: Black Inc., 2009).
13 K. Pearse, 'The Queen's Orphan Asylum-New Town', in I. Terry and K. Evans (eds), *Hobart's History: The First Two Hundred Years, Papers and Proceedings of the Conference Held by the Professional Historians Association of Tasmania on 4 October 1997* (North Hobart: Professional Historians Association, 1998), pp. 27–9.
14 TAHO, SWD28, 'Register of Children Admitted and Discharged from the Male and Female Orphan School, 19 March 1828 to 31 July 1863', p. 38.
15 TAHO, CON41/1/28.
16 *Colonial Times,* Hobart, 10 March 1840.
17 TAHO, NS876/15–27, 'Marriage of Jane Cook and Owen O'Connor, 14 June 1852'.
18 TAHO, AJCP, HO11/16, Reel 92, 'Sentence of Owen, Cornelius, and Thomas Connor, 1848'.
19 TAHO, AJCP, HO11/16, Reel 92, 'Accession Number 2/94, File 2(b), Assignment Lists'.
20 J. Mitchel, *Jail Journal, or Five Years in British Prisons* (Dublin: Gill & Son Ltd., 1913), p. 183.

21 SLNSW, Tasmanian Papers 109, FM4/8516, 'Probation Book from Bermuda to Cape of Good Hope, 5 April 1850'.
22 AJCP, HO11/16, Reel 92; *Tasmanian Government Gazette*, 16 April 1850.
23 Marriage Denis Connor to Margaret McQuin, 29 June 1859, Diocese Kerry, Parish of Tralee, RC (www.irishgenealogy.ie/index.html, 17 March 2012).
24 TAHO, 'Valuation Rolls for the District of Franklin, 1858', p. 8.
25 J. Purtscher, *Father John Murphy's 'Saddlebag' Records, Catholic Baptisms Huon District 1855–1864* (Hobart: I. Schaffer, 1995).
26 TAHO, RGD35/1/40, No. 160, 'Deaths in District of Franklin, Eugene Connors, 17 May 1871'.
27 TAHO, POL377/1, 'Huon Police Charge Book, Franklin, January 1860 to September 1879'.
28 CON41/1/28.
29 Death of Johanna Elliott, M1088 Melbourne, Victoria, 'born Tasmania. Since childhood in Victoria. A few years in Tasmania'.
30 TAHO, CON41/1/28; POL377/1.
31 TAHO, Reg. No. 1534, Reel 35/10, 'Death of Jane Young, 14 Sept. 1890'.
32 TAHO, NS1051/42, 'Burial of Jane Young, Cornelian Bay, Hobart, site A205, 19 September 1890'.
33 Public Records Office Northern Ireland [hereafter, PRONI], Anglesey Papers: D/619/7/1/25-52, 'Rentals 1688–1811, 1760, Patrick McIlreavy and partners'.
34 PRONI, D619/7/1/25, 'Rentals 1766, Pat McElkevy, Owen Hagan and partner'.
35 PRONI, D619/4/72, 'Lease 1769, Patrick, Hugh and Henry McIlrevey'.
36 PRONI, D619/3/9 1784 survey.
37 PRONI, D/619/7/2/59, 'Rent Roll 1845–6, Annual Rentals of the estates of the Most Noble Marquis of Anglesey'.
38 G.C.H.V. Paget, Marquess of Anglesey, *One Leg: The Life and Letters of Henry William Paget, First Marquess of Anglesey, K.G. 1768–1854* (London: Leo Cooper, 1996), pp. 325–6.
39 Ibid. pp. 316–17.
40 Baptism of Mary Caulfield McAleavy, 8 Sept. 1846, Douglas, Isle of Man (www.iomfhs.im/resources/births/dissenter.html). Douglas, Isle of Man, Census records: as Hugh and Sarah McLeod in 1851. Also, Deaths: Hugh & Sarah McAlevey 1871, Douglas, IOM. Grave 2460, Braddon Cemetery.
41 University College Dublin, National Folklore Collection 1957, MS Collection Michael J. Murphy, vol. 1502, Tom MaGee of Drummullagh, p. 200.
42 Ibid. Anne O'Hanlon, p. 40.
43 Paget, *One Leg*, pp. 326–7.
44 PRONI, Anglesey Papers, D619/7/2/61. 'Rent Roll, 1848, Annual Rentals of the estates of the Most Noble Marquis of Anglesey, 1810–1855'.
45 PRONI, D619/7/2/62. 'Rent Roll, 1849'.
46 PRONI, D619/7/2/63. 'Rent Roll, 1850'.
47 *Dundalk Democrat & People's Journal*, 5 January 1850.
48 PRONI, D619/7/2/64. 'Rent Roll, 1851'.
49 Paget, *One Leg*, pp. 327–8.
50 PRONI, D619/7/2/66. 'Rent Rolls, 1853'.

Contributors

Nigel Agnew is a minister in the Reformed Presbyterian Church of Ireland, in Newry. He graduated in law and accounting and was a solicitor before entering Theological College.

Michael Blanch was a taxi driver in Dublin who founded the Committee for the Commemoration of Irish Famine Victims (CCIFV). He was the prime mover in the creation and establishment of the National Famine Memorial Day.

Dr Patrick Fitzgerald is a lecturer and development officer with the Mellon Centre for Migration Studies at the Ulster American Folk Park.

Dr Jason King works with the Irish Heritage Trust. He was previously a lecturer at the University of Limerick and an Assistant Professor of Canadian Irish Studies at Concordia University, Montreal.

Professor Christine Kinealy is a specialist in nineteenth-century Irish history and is currently Professor of History and Director of Ireland's Great Hunger Institute at Quinnipac University, Connecticut.

Lyn McLeavy is an oral historian, writer and photographer from Melbourne, living in Hobart, Tasmania. She told her great-great-grandmother's story in the four-part documentary *Mná Díbeartha* (*Banished Women*), broadcast on the public service Irish language channel, TG4.

Hugh McShane was a graduate of Queen's University Belfast and University of Ulster at Jordanstown, and a former Vice Principal and Head of History and Politics in Sacred Heart Grammar School, Newry, County Down.

John O'Driscoll is the General Manager of Strokestown Park, Ireland's National Famine Museum. He works with the Irish Heritage Trust in safeguarding the Mahon Archive and in organising the annual International Famine Conference.

Professor Cormac Ó Gráda is Professor Emeritus, University College Dublin. His main research interest is the economic histories of Ireland and England and the history of the Great Famine.

Cathal Póirtéir is an award-winning broadcaster and writer who has been broadcasting on RTÉ Radio 1 for thirty years. He has a particular interest in traditional song, social history and literature in the Irish language and has published widely on the folk memory and folklore of the Great Famine.

Dr James Quinn is the managing editor of the Royal Irish Academy's *Dictionary of Irish Biography*. He has written widely on various aspects of Irish nationalism, biography and historiography.

Dr Ciarán Reilly is a research fellow at the Centre for the Study of Historic Irish Houses and Estates. His research interests include the impact of the Great Famine on the landed estate and the country house.

Anthony Russell is retired from Anglia Ruskin University. He is an academic adviser to the annual D'Arcy McGee Summer School and a member of the assessment panel for the Flaherty Research Scholarships.

Index